Kelley Wingate
Reading Comprehension and Skills

Third Grade

Credits
Content Editor: Shirley Pearson
Copy Editor: Elise Craver

Visit *carsondellosa.com* for correlations to Common Core, state, national, and Canadian provincial standards.

Carson-Dellosa Publishing, LLC
PO Box 35665
Greensboro, NC 27425 USA
carsondellosa.com

ISBN 978-1-4838-0494-1
05-327151151

Table of Contents

Introduction 3

Common Core State Standards
Alignment Chart.............................4

Reading Comprehension: Literature

Drawing Conclusions 5

Predicting.................................14

Reading Comprehension: Nonfiction

Cause and Effect.........................20

Main Idea..................................23

Finding Evidence.........................35

Vocabulary.................................41

Point of View 53

Visual Aids.................................59

Writing

Opinion Writing 62

Informative Writing.....................65

Narrative Writing........................68

Language

Word Endings.............................71

Compound Words 80

Homophones 86

Context Clues 95

Answer Key........................104

Introduction

Reading proficiency is as much a result of regular practice as anything. This book was developed to help students practice and master the basic skills necessary to become competent readers.

The skills covered within the activity pages of this book are necessary for successful reading comprehension. Many of the activities will build and reinforce vocabulary, the foundation of reading comprehension. These activities lead to practice with more advanced comprehension skills. Then, students begin to answer comprehension questions based on specific reading passages.

The intent of this book is to strengthen students' foundation in reading basics so that they can advance to more challenging reading work.

Common Core State Standards (CCSS) Alignment

This book supports standards-based instruction and is aligned to the CCSS. The standards are listed at the top of each page for easy reference. To help you meet instructional, remediation, and individualization goals, consult the Common Core State Standards alignment chart on page 4.

Leveled Reading Activities

Instructional levels in this book vary. Each area of the book offers multilevel reading activities so that learning can progress naturally. There are three levels, signified by one, two, or three dots at the bottom of the page:

- Level I: These activities will offer the most support.
- Level II: Some supportive measures are built in.
- Level III: Students will understand the concepts and be able to work independently.

All children learn at their own rate. Use your own judgment for introducing concepts to children when developmentally appropriate.

Hands-On Learning

Review is an important part of learning. It helps to ensure that skills are not only covered but internalized. The flash cards at the back of this book will offer endless opportunities for review. Use them for a basic vocabulary drill, or to play bingo or other fun games.

There is also a certificate template at the back of this book for use as students excel at daily assignments or when they finish a unit.

Common Core State Standards Alignment Chart

Common Core State Standards*		Practice Page(s)
Reading Standards for Literature		
Key Ideas and Details	3.RL.1–3.RL.3	5–19
Craft and Structure	3.RL.4–3.RL.6	7, 71–103
Range of Reading and Level of Text Complexity	3.RL.10	5–19
Reading Standards for Informational Text		
Key Ideas and Details	3.RI.1–3.RI.3	20–61
Craft and Structure	3.RI.4–3.RI.6	41–58
Integration of Knowledge and Ideas	3.RI.7–3.RI.9	59–61
Range of Reading and Level of Text Complexity	3.RI.10	20–61
Reading Standards: Foundational Skills		
Phonics and Word Recognition	3.RF.3	71–79, 86–94
Fluency	3.RF.4	95–103
Writing Standards		
Text Types and Purposes	3.W.1–3.W.3	62–70
Language Standards		
Conventions of Standard English	3.L.1–3.L.2	62–85
Vocabulary Acquisition and Use	3.L.4–3.L.6	62–70, 80–103

Drawing Conclusions

Read the story. Then, answer the questions.

Soup Kitchen

Rashad's parents liked to help other people. His mom made recordings of books for blind people, and his dad built new houses for people who could not afford them. Rashad's mother said that they should have Thanksgiving dinner at the soup kitchen. Rashad's dad said that was an excellent idea. Rashad did not know what a soup kitchen was. He liked soup, so maybe it was a place to try lots of different kinds. But they usually ate turkey and stuffing on Thanksgiving. He did not think that soup would taste as good. On Thanksgiving Day, Rashad helped his dad carry boxes to the car. The boxes held canned goods, fresh vegetables, and even a turkey! When they got to the soup kitchen, Rashad discovered more than just soup. The soup kitchen was a place where people could come for dinner if they had no food of their own. Rashad's parents helped serve dinner. Rashad helped too, and he thought it was the best Thanksgiving he had ever had.

1. How do Rashad's parents help others?

   _____

2. What does Rashad think a soup kitchen is?

   _____

3. What does Rashad's family usually eat on Thanksgiving?

   _____

4. Which clues tell you what a soup kitchen really is?

   _____

   _____

5. How do Rashad's parents help at the soup kitchen?

   _____

6. How can you tell Rashad likes helping people too?

   _____

Drawing Conclusions

Read the story. Then, answer the questions.

Training Jake

Lucy had a playful dog named Jake. He liked to grab her toys and run away from her. When Jake was a puppy, it was easy to catch him. As Jake grew bigger, Lucy had to shout for him to come back. Neither of them was having much fun. Lucy's mom thought Jake should go to obedience training. A trainer could show Lucy how to teach Jake obey her. Lucy found a class that met at the park on Saturday mornings. She walked Jake down to the park, but she felt as if Jake was walking her! He was so strong, she could hardly hold him back. At the park, the other dogs were already sitting politely in a circle. The trainer smiled when Jake and Lucy ran up. The trainer said, "Jake has a lot of energy! I can help both of you learn how to control it."

1. Why is Jake's behavior becoming a problem as he gets bigger?

   _____

   _____

2. Which clues tell you that training will be good for both Jake and Lucy?

   _____

3. When and where does the class meet?

   _____

4. Why does Lucy feel as if Jake is walking her?

   _____

5. How can you tell the other dogs already know some commands?

6. Will the trainer be able to help Jake? Why or why not?

   _____

Drawing Conclusions

Read the story. Then, answer the questions.

A Painting for Mom

Mario loved to paint. He was always asking Mom for money to spend on supplies like brushes and special paper. Sometimes, Mom said that Mario had an expensive talent. Mario was walking home one day when he saw a sign about a city art contest. The topic was "What My Mom Means to Me." The winner would receive a cash prize! Mario thought about all of the art supplies he could buy if he won. As soon as he got home, he got out his paints and brushes. He thought about everything Mom did for their family. She cooked healthy food for him and his sister. She drove them to swimming classes in the summer. She worked hard so that they could buy new shoes when they grew out of their old ones. Mario smiled and started to paint. Now, he had a new idea for what to do with the money if he won.

1. What is Mario doing?

_____

2. Why does Mom say Mario's art talent is expensive?

_____

3. What will the winner of the art contest receive?

_____

4. What does Mario want to do with the prize money?

_____

5. What does Mom do for Mario's family?

_____

_____

6. What might be Mario's new idea for the money at the end of the story?

_____

Drawing Conclusions

Read the story. Then, answer the questions.

Family Photos

Malia's father had accepted a new job across the country. He would be leaving soon. Malia and her mother would be staying in their old house until school was out. Malia would miss her friends when they moved, but she would miss her dad more. Her mother pretended to be cheerful, but Malia knew she would be lonely too. Sometimes, she caught her mom looking at old photos with a tear in her eye. Malia decided to make something that would remind both her mom and her dad that they had a strong family. One afternoon, Malia took the box of family photos up to her room. She cut out two large cardboard hearts. Then, she picked out pictures of herself, her mom, and her dad. She glued the pictures to the hearts. At the top of each heart she wrote "A Family Is Love." Now, Dad would have pictures to remember them by, and Mom would not be so sad when she looked at the photos.

1. Why is Malia's father moving without her and her mom?

   _____

   _____

2. Who will Malia miss the most?

   _____

3. Why does Mom pretend to be cheerful?

   _____

4. Which clues tell you that Mom is not really cheerful?

   _____

5. Why does Malia cut out two cardboard hearts?

   _____

   _____

6. Why will Mom be less sad when she looks at photos now?

   _____

Drawing Conclusions

Read the story. Then, answer the questions.

Alicia's Song

Alicia had been practicing for weeks. She sang in the shower, in her bedroom, and on the way to school. Her teacher said that she was ready to sing in a concert, but Alicia was not sure. Mom had taken her to buy a new dress. She helped Alicia curl her hair. Alicia thought she would feel calm when she walked out onstage, but her palms were sweaty, and her shoes felt too tight. She hoped she would not forget the words. Alicia heard the applause for the performer before her. Her friend Chelsea walked off the stage and whispered, "You're on!" Chelsea patted Alicia's shoulder and said, "Good luck!" Alicia took a deep breath and walked into the spotlight. Finally, it was time for her solo. She saw Mom and her teacher smiling at her from the front row and knew she would do well.

1. What is Alicia doing?

_____

2. How long has Alicia been practicing?

_____

3. Which clues tell you how Alicia feels?

_____

_____

4. How did Mom help Alicia prepare?

_____

5. What does Chelsea do to help Alicia?

_____

6. How does Alicia feel at the end of the story? How do you know?

_____

_____

Drawing Conclusions

Read the story. Then, answer the questions.

Dad's Day

Dad's birthday was in June, near Father's Day. Sometimes, they were even on the same day. Isabelle and Hector thought it was unfair when their dad only had one special day in June. Their friends' dads had Father's Day parties in June and birthday parties in different months. Isabelle thought of a way to fix this problem. They would surprise Dad in autumn with Dad's Day. Hector talked to their mom about cooking a special breakfast. She showed him how to cook eggs and bacon. Isabelle made a special card for Dad. They were careful to keep their plans secret. One day in October, Isabelle and Hector woke up early and crept downstairs. They cooked Dad's breakfast and took it upstairs with their card. Dad loved his surprise. He said that he hoped they could have Dad's Day every weekend!

1. Why do Isabelle and Hector want to have a Dad's Day?

   _____

   _____

2. Why are Dad's birthday and Father's Day on the same day only sometimes?

   _____

3. What does Hector do to prepare?

   _____

4. What does Isabelle do to prepare?

   _____

5. Why do Isabelle and Hector keep their plans secret?

   _____

   _____

6. Why does Dad want to have Dad's Day every weekend?

   _____

Drawing Conclusions

Read the story. Then, answer the questions.

Lamar's Tomato Garden

One day, Lamar's class took a field trip to a greenhouse. The students were amazed at how many different plants were growing in the building. They saw plump tomatoes and lovely pink orchids. The gardener explained that she kept the greenhouse warm and misty so that the plants could grow better. She said that it was easier to grow plants inside the greenhouse, where they were not in danger from bad weather or pests. When Lamar got home from school, he told his mother all about the greenhouse. He asked if they could build one in their backyard. Wouldn't it be great to have fresh tomatoes year-round? Mom said, "A greenhouse sounds like fun, but it can be a lot of work. Why don't you grow some tomatoes in a pot first to see if you have a green thumb." Lamar decided to try. He would grow so many tomatoes that they would need a greenhouse to hold them all!

1. What kinds of plants did Lamar's class see?

_____

2. Why are greenhouses good places to grow plants?

_____

_____

3. What does Lamar want to do?

_____

4. What does Mom suggest?

_____

5. What does it mean to have a green thumb?

_____

6. What does Lamar decide to do at the end of the story?

_____

_____

Predicting

Read each story. Then, answer the questions.

Sandra's mother offered to help her get ready for the new school year. Sandra had grown a full inch taller over the summer. Her shoes were too tight, and her pants were almost above her ankles.

1. What do you think Sandra and her mother will do?

   _____

2. Which clues helped you decide?

   _____

   _____

When Ahmad got home from school, he could not find his cat. Ahmad called out his cat's name, but his cat did not come. Ahmad looked in his closet. He looked under his bed. Just then, Ahmad heard his mom drive up. She was home from work. Ahmad was glad his mom was home.

3. What do you think Ahmad will do?

   _____

4. Which clues helped you decide?

   _____

   _____

Mandy tried out for the school track team. She wore her favorite shoes and came in first in her race. The gym teacher posted the results the day after the tryouts. Mandy raced to the gym to see the list of who had made the team.

5. What do you think will happen next?

   _____

6. Which clues helped you decide?

   _____

Predicting

Read each story. Then, answer the questions.

Miguel needed to write a book report. He finished reading the book and began to plan his paper. The report was worth two test grades, so it was important for him to do well. Miguel's mom said that he had a phone call. It was his friend Tony, who wanted to play video games.

1. What do you think will happen next?

_____

2. Which clues helped you decide?

_____

_____

Yuri laid his head on his desk. His face felt hot, and the desk was nice and cool. Yuri's class was supposed to have an ice cream party that afternoon. Yuri thought the ice cream would feel good to his sore throat. Just then, his teacher said that she thought Yuri should go to the nurse's office.

3. What do you think will happen next?

_____

4. Which clues helped you decide?

_____

_____

Tia and her brother Trey decided to go hiking. They wore sturdy shoes and light clothing. They put on hats and plenty of sunscreen. They had just reached the top of a tall, rocky hill when they heard a clap of thunder. The sky grew dark. Trey spotted a cave in the side of the hill.

5. What do you think will happen next?

_____

6. Which clues helped you decide?

_____

_____

Predicting

Read each story. Then, answer the questions.

Amy's teacher told the class to close their math books. They were having a pop test! Amy was surprised. She was happy that she had studied the chapter the night before. She had not understood the problems in class, so she had asked her mother for extra help. Amy took out a sheet of paper and wrote her name at the top.

1. What do you think will happen next?

_____

2. Which clues helped you decide?

_____

Seth came home from school and prepared himself a sandwich. He put some slices of meat and cheese on it with extra mustard. Seth put his sandwich on a plate and took it to the living room. He thought he would watch his favorite TV show while he ate. His dog came in to see what Seth was doing. Seth set his sandwich on the table and went back into the kitchen for a glass of milk.

3. What do you think will happen next?

_____

4. Which clues helped you decide?

_____

Sarah went to her uncle's farm to visit her cousin Kami. Sarah and Kami were the same age and wore the same size. Sometimes, people thought they were twins! Kami wanted to go fishing, so she told Sarah to put on old jeans. Then, Sarah realized she had forgotten her suitcase.

5. What do you think will happen next?

_____

6. Which clues helped you decide?

_____

Predicting

Read each story. Then, answer the questions.

Raul wanted to earn money this summer. He was tired of asking for change to buy comic books and candy. His best friend, Shane, lived next door. Shane and his family were going to be gone all summer. Shane's family could not travel on the airplane with their two dogs.

1. What do you think Raul will do?

_____

_____

2. Which clues helped you decide?

_____

_____

Jan's family was moving to a new town with their orange-and-white cat. Sadly, the cat ran away when they were moving boxes from the truck to the house. Two weeks later, the cat still had not returned. Jan was very sad. She missed her cat. Her new friend Arifa, who lived next door, called Jan one morning to say that she had just seen an orange-and-white cat in her yard.

3. What do you think will happen next?

_____

_____

4. Which clues helped you decide?

_____

_____

Felicia wanted to surprise her mom with a cake. With Grandma's help, she mixed the ingredients and poured the batter into a pan. She turned on the oven and put the pan inside. She set a timer and waited for the cake to bake. Felicia's mom came home early and called, "What is that wonderful smell?"

5. What do you think will happen next?

_____

_____

6. Which clues helped you decide?

_____

_____

Predicting

Read each story. Then, answer the questions.

   Jason stood at the top of the ladder to the diving board. His knees felt wobbly, and his hands were sweaty. He walked out onto the board. It was a long way down. Just then, he heard his sister shout, "Come on, Jason! You can do it!" He took a deep breath.

1. What do you think Jason will do?

   _____

2. Which clues helped you decide?

   _____

   _____

   Quan's father was working late every night. He had not gotten home before dark for the past month. Quan noticed that the yard was covered in dead leaves. He knew his mom did not like it. She had hurt her leg and could not stand up for very long. Quan wanted to help.

3. What do you think Quan will do?

   _____

4. Which clues helped you decide?

   _____

   _____

   Jayla took piano lessons. She liked to play for her mom every night after dinner. Sometimes, her friends came over to sing while she played. Jayla's piano teacher was having a party for all of her students the next week. She wanted all of her students to play for each other, and one would win a prize.

5. What do you think will happen next?

   _____

6. Which clues helped you decide?

   _____

Predicting

Read each story. Then, answer the questions.

   Tara found a pair of sunglasses on the bus. They were bright pink with red lightning bolts on the earpieces. Tara felt like a rock star wearing them. After lunch, Tara put on the sunglasses to go out for recess. An older girl ran up to her and said, "Excuse me, but I think that those are mine." Tara's heart sank.

1. What do you think Tara will do?

   _____

2. Which clues helped you decide?

   _____

   Ray wanted to play football more than anything else in the world. A new team was starting in his neighborhood, and he wanted to try out. His family was concerned that if Ray joined the team, he would not have time to do his homework. His family wanted Ray to have fun, but they also wanted him to do well in school. Ray was sure that he would have time to do his homework and play on the team.

3. What do you think will happen next?

   _____

4. Which clues helped you decide?

   _____

   Ivy's grandmother would be celebrating her 70th birthday soon. Ivy wanted to get her grandmother a special gift, but she had spent her money on new books instead. Ivy loved reading books about Mexico. Her grandmother had come from Mexico, and she used to read to Ivy when she was little. Lately, her grandmother's eyesight had been failing, and she could no longer see the words on the page.

5. What do you think Ivy will do?

   _____

6. Which clues helped you decide?

   _____

   _____

Cause and Effect

Read the story. Then, answer the questions.

Saguaro Cactus

In the Arizona desert, a cactus grows that will live 100 years or more. The saguaro cactus grows very slowly in the hot, dry desert, and it becomes home to many animals as it grows.

The cactus starts as a seed dropped from the fruit of a mature saguaro cactus. The seed sprouts after a rare rain gives it moisture. It swells up, splits its shell, and sends a root down into the soil. Then, the seed sends up a stem.

It does not rain often in the desert, so the stem grows slowly. After one year, it will have grown less than a centimeter. After 10 years, it may be only 15 centimeters (6 inches) tall. When it is 50 years old, the original stem is about 4.5 meters (15 feet) tall. After 50 years, the saguaro cactus finally grows its first branches.

Many animals make their homes in the saguaro cactus. Animals like its moist skin. Animals like woodpeckers, mice, hawks, and owls can live in the cactus.

Beautiful flowers grow on the mature saguaro cactus. The flowers provide juicy nectar for birds, insects, and bats. After the flowers dry up, green fruits cover the cactus. Many animals come to eat the fruit. They spread the seeds from the fruit onto the ground where the seeds wait for rain. Eventually these seeds will sprout and grow new saguaro cacti. The cycle goes will continue for hundreds of years.

1. What causes a saguaro cactus seed to sprout?

_____

2. What causes the cactus stem to grow so slowly?

_____

3. What happens because the cactus has moist skin?

_____

4. What must happen before the seeds can sprout and grow new cacti?

_____

5. Why do you think the cactus grows flowers and fruit?

_____

_____

Cause and Effect

Read the story. Then, answer the questions.

Tepees

For centuries, people have lived on the Great Plains. This is flat grassland with few trees. Many animals used to roam here. People would follow them to hunt. People needed homes they could quickly tear down and set up. Tribes such as the Arapaho, Pawnee, Blackfoot, Sioux, and Cheyenne used tipis. Tepees were made of wood poles and buffalo hides. When buffalo became scarce, Plains people used canvas instead of hides.

The first step in making a tepee was to prepare the poles. They had to be long and straight. The best trees to use were willow, lodgepole pine, and cedar. When people traveled, the poles dragged on the ground. They wore out and had to be replaced.

The women prepared the buffalo hides. First, they scraped each hide. Then, they soaked the hides in water to soften them. Next, they sewed the hides together in the shape of a half circle. They cut a hole for the door and created smoke flaps. Finally, they fitted the cover over the frame and lit a fire inside. The smoke preserved the hide.

In the late 1800s, roads and cities were built. Many of the Plains people were forced to live on reservations. They no longer lived in tepees. Still, the tepee remains an important part of American Indian culture today.

1. What caused the Plains people to move around so much?

    _____

2. How did their lifestyle of moving affect their style of home?

    _____

3. What caused them to use canvas instead of buffalo hides for tepee covers?

    _____

4. What was the effect on the poles when they were dragged on the ground?

    _____

5. What was the effect of water on the buffalo hides?

    _____

6. On a separate sheet of paper, explain why you think it is important to preserve the culture of the Plains people.

Cause and Effect

Read the story. Then, answer the questions.

Yellowstone Fires

In 1988, a huge fire burned nearly half of Yellowstone National Park. This was a healthy part of the forest's natural life cycle. The forest had been growing for centuries. Many trees had died. Their trunks fell on the ground and remained there. Eventually, the ground was covered with dead trees. This blocked the sun from reaching new growth on the forest floor. It also made it difficult for animals to travel. There were fewer meadows for new plants, and animals had less grazing area.

Lightning started several fires that summer. The dead tree trunks on the forest floor ignited like firewood. Firefighters were able to protect some areas from burning but the fires did not stop until snow fell.

After the fires were out, the forests began to grow again. Some roots and seeds had remained safe underground. Others, such as lodgepole pine seeds, had been locked in cones that the heat had released. Beautiful new plants grew. This provided perfect food for the animals. Many of the surviving animals live in the meadows that now cover much of the park. More than half of the park was untouched, so forests still remain.

Yellowstone continues to recover. As the park evolves, new animals and plants find their homes there. In about 300 years, the park will be ready for a new fire to give it a fresh start once again.

1. What is an effect of a fire on trees and plants in a forest?

   _____

2. What is an effect on the forest if fires do not occur for years?

   _____

3. What caused the fires to spread so quickly?

   _____

4. What will be the effect of 300 more years of growth?

   _____

   _____

5. Was the effect of the Yellowstone fires positive or negative? Explain your answer.

   _____

   _____

Main Idea

Read the story. Then, answer the questions.

Martin Luther King Jr.

Martin Luther King Jr. was an important leader in the US civil rights movement. This movement forced leaders to change unfair laws so that all people would be treated fairly, regardless of their skin color. King was born in 1929 in Atlanta, Georgia. In 1954, King became the leader of a church in Montgomery, Alabama. During this time, African Americans were told that they had to give up their bus seats if white people wanted to sit. King and others refused to ride the buses at all until they were given equal treatment. In 1963, he led a march in Washington, DC, to ask the government to change the laws so that everyone was treated fairly. King received the Nobel Peace Prize in 1964 for his work. He traveled to Memphis, Tennessee, in 1968 to give a speech in support of equal wages. He was shot on April 4, 1968. Although King died, his ideas on freedom and equality live on today.

1. What is the main idea of this story?

   a. Martin Luther King Jr. was a great civil rights leader.

   b. Martin Luther King Jr. led a march in 1963.

   c. Martin Luther King Jr. was born in 1929.

2. Why did King lead a march in Washington, D.C.?

   _____

   _____

3. Circle the correct word in parentheses to complete each sentence.

   a. King led a march to Washington, D.C. (after, before) he became the leader of a church in Montgomery, Alabama.

   b. King received the Nobel Peace Prize (after, before) he traveled to Memphis, Tennessee to give an important speech.

   c. King was shot (after, before) he gave his speech in support of equal wages.

4. Why do you think King received the Nobel Peace Prize in 1964? On a separate sheet of paper, write a paragraph explaining your opinion.

Main Idea

Read the story. Then, answer the questions.

James Naismith

Have you ever played basketball with your friends? You dribble the ball, run down the court, and shoot the ball through a hoop. The modern game of basketball was invented by James Naismith in 1891. Naismith was a Canadian gym teacher. He wanted a game that would not take up too much room. He wanted to be able to play it indoors. Naismith nailed peach baskets at both ends of the gym. Then, he sorted his players into two teams of nine each. The players passed a ball to each other. Then, they threw it into the basket when they reached the end of the court. Eventually, players started to bounce the ball instead of just tossing it to each other. This bouncing motion became known as dribbling. Basketball soon caught on among both men's and women's teams. It became an official Olympic sport in 1936, and Naismith was invited to watch. Naismith died in 1939, but his sport lives on. Over 300 million people around the world play basketball today.

1. What is the main idea of this story?

   a. James Naismith's sport lives on today.

   b. James Naismith was a gym teacher.

   c. James Naismith invented the sport of basketball.

2. What did the first basketball hoops look like?

   _____

3. What kind of game did Naismith want to invent?

   _____

4. Circle the correct word in parentheses to complete each sentence.

   a. Naismith invented basketball (after, before) 1908.

   b. Basketball became an Olympic sport (after, before) Naismith died.

   c. In the original basketball game, players passed the ball to each other directly (after, before) they threw the ball into the basket.

5. Do you think basketball is still popular today? On a separate sheet of paper, write a paragraph explaining your opinion.

Main Idea

Read the story. Then, answer the questions.

Lucy Maud Montgomery

Lucy Maud Montgomery was a famous Canadian author. Her most beloved character is Anne Shirley in the widely read series Anne of Green Gables. Montgomery was born in 1874 on Prince Edward Island. She lived with her grandparents. Montgomery went to class in a one-room schoolhouse. At age 17, her first poem was published. Montgomery taught at three island schools. She took courses at a university in nearby Nova Scotia. Montgomery wrote *Anne of Green Gables* in 1905. It was not published until 1908. The book became a best seller. Montgomery wrote several other books based on the main character. Two films and at least seven TV shows have been made from the Anne books. Although Montgomery moved away in 1911, all but one of her books is set in Prince Edward Island. Many people today still visit the island to see where "Anne Shirley" grew up.

1. What is the main idea of this story?

    a. Lucy Maud Montgomery grew up on Prince Edward Island.

    b. Lucy Maud Montgomery is famous for writing *Anne of Green Gables*.

    c. Lucy Maud Montgomery was a schoolteacher.

2. Who is Anne Shirley?

    _____

    _____

3. Why do you think *Anne of Green Gables* was a popular book?

    _____

4. Circle the correct word in parentheses to complete each sentence.

    a. *Anne of Green Gables* was published (after, before) Montgomery moved away from Prince Edward Island.

    b. Montgomery lived with her grandparents (before, while) attending university in Nova Scotia.

    c. Montgomery's first poem was published (after, before) 1905.

5. Why do you think many people visit Prince Edward Island today? On a separate sheet of paper, write a paragraph explaining your opinion.

Main Idea

Read the story. Then, answer the questions.

Amelia Earhart

Amelia Earhart was a famous airplane pilot. She was the first woman to fly across the Atlantic Ocean. Earhart was born in 1897. She saw her first airplane at the Iowa state fair at age 10. Earhart studied to be a nurse and then a social worker. But, she was always interested in flight. She started taking flying lessons in 1921. The first airplane Earhart bought was bright yellow. She called it Canary. In 1928, Earhart flew from Canada to Wales. She crossed the Atlantic Ocean in only 21 hours. When she returned to the United States, a parade was held in her honor. Earhart crossed the Atlantic again in 1932. This time, she flew by herself. The U.S. Congress gave her a special medal for this accomplishment. The medal is called the Distinguished Flying Cross. Earhart continued to set new records. In 1937, she decided to fly around the world. Her airplane was lost over the Pacific Ocean. Amelia Earhart was never heard from again.

1. What is the main idea of this story?

   a. Amelia Earhart flew around the world.

   b. Amelia Earhart was a brave woman who flew airplanes.

   c. Amelia Earhart had a yellow airplane called Canary.

2. Why do you think Earhart called her first airplane Canary?

   _____

3. You can tell a lot about people by what they do. Circle the adjective(s) that you think describe Amelia Earhart. Use a dictionary if necessary.

   adventurous   timid   popular   determined

4. What do you think happened to Earhart in 1937? Use an encyclopedia, the Internet, and maps to learn about that area in the Pacific Ocean. On a separate sheet of paper, write a paragraph explaining your opinion.

Main Idea

Read the story. Then, answer the questions.

Roberto Clemente

Roberto Clemente was born in Puerto Rico in 1934. As a child, he played baseball in his neighborhood. He also played for his high school team. At 16, he joined a junior national league. He played baseball briefly in Canada before signing to play for the Pittsburgh Pirates in 1954. Clemente served in the US Marine Reserves for several years. This helped him grow physically stronger. He later helped the Pirates win two World Series. During the off-season, Clemente often went back to Puerto Rico to help. He liked visiting children in hospitals. He gave them hope that they could get well. In 1972, an earthquake hit the country of Nicaragua. Clemente helped there too. He was on his way to deliver supplies to Nicaragua when he died in an airplane crash. He was 38 years old. Clemente was elected to the Baseball Hall of Fame in 1973. He was the first Hispanic player to receive the honor.

1. What is the main idea of this story?

    a. Roberto Clemente was a great baseball player who also helped people.

    b. Roberto Clemente died in a plane crash.

    c. Roberto Clemente was elected to the Baseball Hall of Fame.

2. You can tell a lot about people by what they do. Circle the adjective(s) that you think describe Roberto Clemente. Use a dictionary if necessary.

    athletic   caring   persistent   selfish

3. Circle the correct word in parentheses to complete each sentence.

    a. Clemente served in the US Marine Reserves (after, before) he played baseball in Canada.

    b. Clemente's team won the World Series (before, after) he was voted into the Baseball Hall of Fame.

    c. The airplane crash occurred (after, before) the Venezuelan earthquake.

4. What visual aids (e.g., maps, photographs) would help you better understand this story? Why?

_____

5. Clemente helped with relief efforts in the Central American country of Nicaragua. If you were famous, do you think you would want to help in that way? Why or why not? On a separate sheet of paper, write a paragraph explaining your opinion.

Main Idea

Read the story. Then, answer the questions.

Titanic

In the spring of 1912, the *Titanic* set off from England. This was its first journey. The *Titanic* was a luxury ship headed for New York City. But, its journey across the icy Atlantic Ocean was cut short. Around midnight on April 14, the ship hit an iceberg. In less than three hours the ship had sunk. Over 700 people survived. However, more than 1,500 lives were lost. Because of the way the *Titanic* was built, everyone thought it was impossible for the ship to sink. This certainty led to several of the causes of the disaster. We now know that the captain had ignored warnings of ice. He pushed the *Titanic* too fast through dangerous waters. We also know that there were not enough lifeboats on board. Because of the *Titanic* disaster, new rules were set. Now people know that every ship can sink, so ships must carry enough lifeboats for everyone on board.

1. What is the main idea of this story?

   a. The *Titanic* was unsinkable.

   b. The sinking of the *Titanic* was a huge disaster.

   c. A ship called the *Titanic* left England in 1912.

2. What does the phrase *cut short* in this story mean?

   _____

3. What does the story say contributed to, or caused, the disaster?

   _____

4. Circle the correct word in parentheses to complete each sentence.

   a. The *Titanic* sank (after, before) it left England.

   b. The captain received warnings of ice (after, before) the *Titanic* hit an iceberg.

   c. Over 700 people aboard the *Titanic* survived (after, before) the ship sank.

5. What visual aids (e.g., maps, photographs) would help you better understand this story? Why?

   _____

6. What do you think might have happened if the *Titanic* had provided enough lifeboats for everyone? On a separate sheet of paper, write a paragraph explaining your opinion.

Main Idea

Read the story. Then, answer the questions.

Thomas Jefferson

Thomas Jefferson was an important figure in early US history. He was born in 1743 in the colony of Virginia. He became a lawyer. Jefferson grew active in the government of the new country that would become the United States. In 1776, he helped write the US Declaration of Independence. This document said that the American colonies were no longer tied to Great Britain. Jefferson served as governor of Virginia. Then, he went to France to help strengthen ties between the two countries. Jefferson became the third president of the United States. He served two terms from 1801 to 1809. During his presidency, Jefferson authorized the Louisiana Purchase. This agreement expanded US territory to include over 800,000 square miles (207,200,000 square km) from Canada to the Gulf Coast. Jefferson died in 1826. Americans are reminded of him every time they spend a nickel. Jefferson's face is on one side. His home, Monticello, is on the other.

1. What is the main idea of this story?

    a. Thomas Jefferson was an important person in US history.

    b. Thomas Jefferson's face is on the nickel.

    c. Thomas Jefferson was a lawyer.

2. You can tell a lot about people by what they say and do. Which sentence may have been said by Thomas Jefferson?

    a. "I love living in a British colony."

    b. "I don't think we should make this country any bigger."

    c. "I think friends and allies are important for a country."

    d. "I wrote the Declaration of Independence in about 10 minutes."

3. Which of the following sentences are true?

    a. Jefferson became president after 1800.

    b. The Declaration of Independence was written before the Louisiana Purchase occurred.

    c. Jefferson became governor of Virginia after he became a lawyer.

    d. Jefferson went to France before 1743.

4. Use resource books or the Internet to learn about the Louisiana Purchase. How did the Louisiana Purchase change the United States? Use a computer to type your research paper.

Main Idea

Read the story. Then, answer the questions.

Babe Didrikson Zaharias

Babe Didrikson Zaharias was an outstanding sportswoman. She played golf, basketball, and baseball and also ran track. Zaharias grew up playing sports with her six brothers and sisters in Port Arthur, Texas. She played basketball on a company team when she worked as a secretary. She joined the US Olympic team and won medals in three track-and-field events at the 1932 Olympics in Los Angeles. Zaharias began playing golf in 1935, and in 1938 she became the first woman to play in a PGA (Professional Golf Association) game. She became famous for her playing, and in 1950 she helped form the LPGA (Ladies Professional Golf Association). This group continues to hold golf matches for female golfers today. Zaharias died in 1956, but she was named to the US Olympic Hall of Fame in 1983. People can learn more about Zaharias's life by visiting a museum in her honor in Beaumont, Texas.

1. What is the main idea of this story?

   a. Babe Didrikson Zaharias grew up in Texas.

   b. Babe Didrikson Zaharias was good at many sports.

   c. Babe Didrikson Zaharias died in 1956.

2. What happened to Zaharias at the 1932 Olympics?

   _____

3. In the sentence "This group continues to hold golf matches for female golfers today," what does the word *hold* mean?

   a. grab with their hands   b. arrange

   c. rest   d. stop

4. You can tell a lot about people by what they say and do. Which sentence may have been said by Babe Didrikson Zaharias?

   a. "I don't feel like exercising today."

   b. "It doesn't matter if you're a girl or a boy."

   c. "I would prefer to play a board game."

   d. "I'd much rather tie than win."

5. Use resource books or the Internet to learn about the LPGA. What does the LPGA do today? Use a computer to type your research paper.

Main Idea

Read the story. Then, answer the questions.

Louisa May Alcott

For nearly 150 years, children have grown up reading about the March sisters. Meg, Jo, Beth, and Amy March are characters in the famous book *Little Women*. *Little Women* was written by Louisa May Alcott. Alcott grew up with three sisters in Massachusetts. In the book, the March sisters like to put on plays for their friends. Alcott and her sisters liked to do the same! Alcott's family was very poor. She helped them by working at many jobs. She was a maid, a teacher, a nurse, and a writer. Her books about the March family start with *Little Women*. These books were widely read during Alcott's lifetime. The main character, Jo, is based on Alcott herself. Jo works as a writer until she marries and has a family. Alcott continued to write until her death in 1888. She also spoke out for her beliefs. She supported women's rights. She was against slavery. Today, people can visit Orchard House, the home where Alcott grew up. It is also the place where *Little Women* is set.

1. What is the main idea of this story?

   a. Louisa May Alcott was very poor as a child.

   b. Louisa May Alcott had three sisters.

   c. Louisa May Alcott based her books on her own life.

2. What was Alcott known for besides writing?

   _____

3. In the sentence "These books were widely read during Alcott's lifetime," what does the phrase *widely read* mean?

   a. read by few people   b. taking up a lot of space

   c. not thin   d. read by many people

4. You can tell a lot about people by what they say and do. Which sentence may have been said by Louisa May Alcott?

   a. "I've run out of ideas on how to help my family."   b. "I'll buy the best that you have!"

   c. "All people are created equal."   d. "Why do I have to help?"

5. Use resource books or the Internet to learn about Louisa May Alcott and her family, and the March sisters from *Little Women*. Compare the Alcott family with the fictional March family. Use a computer to type your research paper.

Main Idea

Read the story. Then, answer the questions.

Wayne Gretzky

Wayne Gretzky is called "The Great One" by fans of Canadian hockey. He scored over 1,000 goals during his career. Gretzky was born in Brantford, Ontario. He learned to ice-skate on his family's farm when he was three. Gretzky's father taught him and his three brothers to play hockey. They played on a frozen pond in the backyard. When Gretzky was six, he joined a league of 10-year-olds and began playing on a team. In the summer, he played baseball and lacrosse. His first professional hockey team was the Indianapolis Racers. He played for them when he was only 17. Then, he played for the Edmonton Oilers in Canada for nine years. During this time, they won hockey's Stanley Cup four times. He also played for several US teams. Gretzky retired from the sport in 1999. He was voted into the Hockey Hall of Fame. Both his hometown of Brantford and his adopted city of Edmonton named streets after Gretzky to honor him.

1. What is the main idea of this story?

   a. Wayne Gretzky was a great hockey player.

   b. Wayne Gretzky had three brothers.

   c. Wayne Gretzky played hockey in the United States and Canada.

2. Where did Gretzky first play hockey?

   _____

3. What does the story say caused the Edmonton Oilers to win the Stanley Cup so many times?

   _____

4. Fans call Wayne Gretzky "The Great One" or "The Great Gretzky." Great Gretzky is an example of an *alliteration* which means the same sounds are repeated in nearby words. If Gretzky's name had been "Smith," people might have called him "Super Smith." On a separate sheet of paper, write the names of three people you admire. For each person, create at least two alliterations that show your admiration. Use any or all parts of their names. Write a sentence explaining each alliteration.

Main Idea

Read the story. Then, answer the questions.

Lady Bird Johnson

Lady Bird Johnson was born as Claudia Taylor in 1912. A nurse said that Claudia was as pretty as a ladybird beetle. Ladybird is another name for a ladybug. So, Lady Bird became her nickname. Lady Bird married Lyndon Baines Johnson in 1934. Together, they had two daughters. In 1963, President John F. Kennedy was killed. Lyndon Johnson became president of the United States. Lady Bird became the First Lady. Most women who serve as first lady choose a special project to work on. Lady Bird chose highway beautification. She wanted to make the highways of the United States more beautiful. She helped get millions of flowers planted. We can still see these flowers today. Lady Bird believed that "where flowers bloom, so does hope." She continued to help make her home state of Texas more beautiful after her husband left office. The Lady Bird Johnson Wildflower Center in Austin, Texas, was opened to help visitors learn about native plants.

1. What is the main idea of this story?

   a. Lady Bird Johnson was born in 1912.

   b. Lady Bird Johnson was married to a president.

   c. Lady Bird Johnson helped make America's highways beautiful.

2. How did Lady Bird get her nickname?

   _____

3. How did Lady Bird become the first lady?

   _____

   _____

4. Lady Bird believed that "where flowers bloom, so does hope." Did Lady Bird really believe that hope grew from a seed in the ground? Explain your answer.

   _____

   _____

5. Use an encyclopedia or the Internet to learn about he Lady Bird Johnson Wildflower Center. What does this center do? On a separate sheet of paper, write a paragraph to tell about the Wildflower Center.

Main Idea

Read the story. Then, answer the questions.

Edward R. Murrow

Edward R. Murrow was an American journalist. He was born in 1908 in North Carolina. After college, Murrow began working for a radio station. He became famous during World War II. In September 1939, London, England, was bombed. This was known as the Blitz. Murrow was there! People all over America listened to his live broadcasts. Americans used to learn about the war only through newsreels in movie theaters or newspaper articles. Now, they could listen to Murrow on their radios at home. Murrow was very brave to risk his life so that Americans could learn about the war in London. When the war ended, Murrow continued to work as a radio reporter. Then, he moved to television. On TV, he became known for interviewing. He would interview, or ask questions of, famous people. Other newscasters followed in Murrow's footsteps. Today, we still look forward to hearing from reporters in other countries. We can even listen in on their chats with famous people!

1. What is the main idea of this story?

    a. Edward R. Murrow was a brave American journalist.

    b. Edward R. Murrow talked to many famous people.

    c. Edward R. Murrow worked in London.

2. What type of company did Murrow work for?

    _____

3. What was special about Murrow's broadcasts in 1939?

    _____

4. How did people learn about the war before Murrow's work?

    _____

5. What does the story say caused modern reporters to interview famous people?

    _____

6. Pretend you are a reporter. Ask someone for permission to be the subject of your interview. Prepare by writing a number of questions in advance. Leave enough room after each question to record the answer. Choose a way to publish and share your interview.

Finding Evidence

Read the story. Then, answer the questions. Underline evidence in the story that supports your answers.

Elisha Otis

Have you ever ridden on an elevator? Elevators make it much easier for people to get from one floor to another in a tall building. At one time, elevators were not as safe as they are today. Elisha Otis helped change that. Early elevators used ropes. These ropes sometimes broke, sending the people riding the elevator to the ground. People could be hurt. Otis made wooden guide rails to go on each side of the elevator. Cables ran through the rails. The cables were connected to a spring that would pull the elevator back up if the cables broke. Otis displayed his invention for the first time at the New York Crystal Palace Exhibition in 1853. His safety elevators were used in buildings as tall as the Eiffel Tower in Paris, France, and the Empire State Building in New York City. Otis died in 1861. His sons, Charles and Norton, continued to sell his design, and many elevators today still have the Otis name on them.

1. What is the main idea of this story?

   a. The Otis family still sells elevators today.

   b. At one time, elevators were unsafe to use.

   c. Elisha Otis found a way to make elevators safe.

2. What are two buildings that used Otis's elevator design?

   _____

3. You can tell a lot about people by what they say and do. Which sentence may have been said by Elisha Otis?

   a. "I have an idea."

   b. "Don't bother. It's probably good enough."

   c. "Just take the stairs."

   d. "Ropes are just as strong as cable."

4. Think of the times you have been in an elevator. Write a letter to Otis to thank him for making elevators safe. Describe some of the places where you have used an elevator. Use a computer to type your letter.

Finding Evidence

Read the story. Then, answer the questions. Underline evidence in the passage that supports your answers.

Susan B. Anthony

You may know the name Susan B. Anthony from the US dollar coin. But, Anthony was famous long before the coin was made. She was a leader who worked for women's rights in the nineteenth and twentieth centuries. Anthony grew up in the Northeast of the United States. A teacher refused to teach her math because she was a girl. So, Anthony was educated at home. She became a teacher and fought for equal wages for women. Anthony attended a special meeting in New York, along with many others. She then began speaking publicly about women's rights. In 1869, Anthony and Elizabeth Cady Stanton formed a group. This was called the National Women's Suffrage Association. This group worked to gain women the right to vote. Anthony died in 1906. In 1920, the Nineteenth Amendment to the US Constitution was passed. This finally gave American women the right to vote. Anthony was honored in 1979 with a dollar coin bearing her image.

1. What is the main idea of this story?

    a. Susan B. Anthony could not learn to do math.

    b. Susan B. Anthony worked for women's rights.

    c. A dollar coin honored Susan B. Anthony in 1979.

2. Why was Anthony educated at home?

    _____

3. What did Anthony fight for as a teacher?

    _____

4. You can tell a lot about people by what they say and do. Which sentence may have been said by Susan B. Anthony?

    a. "We'll never be able to change the law."

    b. "Come on, ladies! This is our right!"

    c. "This is the way it has always been, so this is the way it should stay."

    d. "I'm so disorganized."

5. Think of the women you know. Think of how life would be different if women did not have the right to vote. Write a letter to Anthony to thank her for her work. Describe some of the women in your life and why you think it is important that they are able to vote. Use a computer to type your letter.

Finding Evidence

Read the story. Then, answer the questions. Underline evidence in the story that supports your answers.

Thomas Edison

Without Thomas Alva Edison, we might all be sitting around in the dark! Although people before Edison worked on designs for the lightbulb, he is credited with creating the modern electric light. Edison was born in 1847. He worked as a telegraph operator. Edison liked working on the night shift so that he could have plenty of time to read and conduct experiments during the day. He invented the phonograph, or record player, in 1877. Edison built his own lab at Menlo Park, New Jersey. There he could continue to work on his inventions. The lab covered the space of two city blocks. Edison showed his lightbulb to the public in 1879. At this time, most people used candles to light their homes. The candles sometimes caused house fires. By 1887, over 100 power plants were sending electricity to customers. Edison registered over 1,000 patents. A patent is a document that gives an inventor the right to make, use, or sell an invention. It is no wonder that a newspaper called him the Wizard of Menlo Park!

1. What is the main idea of this story?

   _____

2. What are two of Edison's inventions?

   _____

3. Why did Edison like working on the night shift?

   _____

4. Circle the synonym that best replaces the word *conduct* in the sentence.

   This gave him plenty of time to read and conduct experiments during the day.

   lead   pass   perform   run

5. You can tell a lot about people by what they say and do. Which sentence may *not* have been said by Thomas Edison?

   a. "How about if I try this?"   b. "That might be a better way!"

   c. "I might need more space."   d. "Candlelight is so comforting."

6. Think of how life would be different if the modern lightbulb had not been invented. Write a letter to thank Edison for his invention. Use a computer to type your letter.

Finding Evidence

Read the story. Then, answer the questions. Underline evidence in the story that supports your answers.

Community Helpers

A community is a group of people. These people live in the same area or have the same interests. Communities need helpers to make them work. Some important community helpers are police officers. Police officers make sure everyone is following the rules of the community. They keep people safe. Firefighters are community helpers too. Firefighters put out fires. They also educate people about fire safety. Other community helpers are people who work for the city. Garbage collectors help out. People put trash in bags or cans at the curb. Garbage collectors drive down city streets to pick up the trash. Park rangers help out too. People play or have picnics in city parks. Park rangers make sure the parks are clean and safe. Another important helper in the community is a librarian. The librarian makes sure there are many good books available. Everyone in the community can use the library. The next time you see a community helper say, "Thank you!"

1. What is the main idea of this story?

   a. A community needs a lot of people to make it work.

   b. Police officers and firefighters are community helpers.

   c. People like to have picnics in city parks.

2. What do police officers do in a community?

   _____

   _____

3. Why does a community need park rangers?

   _____

   _____

4. There are many other community helpers. Think of a community helper who has helped you or your family. Write a letter to thank this person. Describe how this person has affected your life. Use a computer to type your letter.

Finding Evidence

Read the story. Then, answer the questions. Underline evidence in the story that supports your answers.

Musical Cultures

People from different cultures celebrate different holidays. They eat different kinds of food. They also have different musical cultures. The United States has many musical traditions. People in New Orleans, Louisiana, in the southern part of the United States, are known for jazz. This music has strong rhythms. Jazz allows people to play freely. People from a region of the eastern United States called Appalachia play folk music with fiddles and banjos. Much of this music is based on the songs and dance tunes of the British Isles. Countries that border each other have music styles from the people who cross from one country to the other. Some styles from Mexico are banda and cumbia. Some Canadian styles of music are based on French songs. These styles use accordions and guitars. Because of radio and TV, people all over the world can hear music of other cultures and create new musical traditions of their own.

1. What is the main idea of this story?

    a. Different cultures have different holidays and food.

    b. Some Canadian music is based on French songs.

    c. People have different musical cultures.

2. What is *jazz*?

    _____

    _____

3. What are some styles of music from Mexico?

    _____

4. How do radio and TV affect musical cultures?

    _____

    _____

5. What is your favorite kind of music? What types of instruments do you like listening to? Do you create music yourself? Write a letter to a famous musician describing what you like about his or her music. Use a computer to type your letter.

Name _____

3.RI.1, 3.RI.2, 3.RI.10

Finding Evidence

Read the story. Then, answer the questions. Underline evidence in the story that supports your answers.

World Holidays

You and your family may celebrate many special days a year. People all over the world recognize different holidays. Some people in China have a Lantern Festival. This festival celebrates the new year. They light special lamps and hold colorful parades through the streets. In Scotland, some people celebrate Burns Night. This holiday honors the Scottish poet Robert Burns. It falls on his birthday. Families or clubs gather to eat a special meal. Then, they read Burn's poetry. Americans celebrate their independence on Independence Day. Canadians celebrate Canada Day on July 1, because the government of Canada was created on that day in 1867. On both Canada Day and Independence Day, people have parades and picnics. People in some parts of Germany celebrate Oktoberfest. This festival marks the harvest. They eat traditional German foods like sausage and potato salad. People who move to other countries carry their traditions to their new homes. This is why many places outside of those countries celebrate the same holidays.

1. What is the main idea of this story?

    a. Burns Night is a special holiday in Scotland.

    b. People around the world celebrate different holidays.

    c. Oktoberfest takes place in many cities.

2. How do people in Scotland honor Robert Burns?

    _____

3. How are Independence Day and Canada Day celebrations alike?

    _____

4. What does Oktoberfest represent?

    _____

5. Why might people take their traditions to new countries?

    _____

6. Think of three holidays that you celebrate. Write a letter to a pen pal from another country describing these holidays. Use a computer to type your letter.

© Carson-Dellosa • CD-104621

Vocabulary

Read the story. Then, answer the questions.

Elijah McCoy

You may have heard something referred to as "the real McCoy." This saying means "the real thing" instead of a copy. Some people think that "the real McCoy" was Elijah McCoy, who was born in Canada in 1843. His parents were former slaves who escaped from Kentucky to Canada. At the time, slavery was illegal in Canada but not in the United States. McCoy traveled to Scotland when he was 16 to learn how to design, build, and repair machines. After the US Civil War ended, he moved to Michigan, where he worked on the railroad. He had to pour oil into the engine whenever the train stopped. McCoy worked on inventions in his home machine shop. He came up with the idea for a device to keep train engines oiled. His invention helped trains run more smoothly. Railroad workers would ask for "the real McCoy" because it was better than other machines like it.

1. What is the main idea of this story?

   a. Elijah McCoy created a tool to keep train engines running smoothly.

   b. Elijah McCoy was "the real McCoy" that the saying refers to.

   c. Elijah McCoy spent several years in Scotland.

2. What does the phrase *the real McCoy* mean?

   _____

3. You can tell a lot about people by what they do. Circle the adjective(s) that you think describe Elijah McCoy. Use a dictionary if necessary.

   fearful   industrious

   innovative   tired

4. Is there something you use that you would want "the real McCoy" for as well? Why? On a separate sheet of paper, describe what you would want. Support your opinion with several reasons.

Vocabulary

Read the story. Then, answer the questions.

Sandford Fleming

What time is it? Before the work of Sandford Fleming, it could be hard to tell. Fleming was born in Scotland in 1827. He moved to Canada to work on the railway. He drew up plans for a railroad from the east coast to the west coast. He worked to promote the use of iron bridges rather than wood. Fleming thought iron bridges were safer. In 1851, he designed the first Canadian postage stamp. It was worth three cents and had a picture of a beaver on it. In 1876, Fleming was traveling in Ireland. He missed his train. The schedule said that it would leave at 11 o'clock in the evening. Instead, the train left at 11 o'clock in the morning. Fleming knew how to avoid this kind of problem. He suggested that countries around the world use a single 24-hour clock. By 1929, most of the world's countries had adopted time zones that fit into this standardized timemeasurement.

1. What is the main idea of this story?

   a. Sandford Fleming was Scottish but lived in Canada.

   b. Sandford Fleming came up with the idea for standardized time.

   c. Sandford Fleming missed a train in Ireland.

2. You can tell a lot about people by what they do. Circle the adjective(s) that you think describe Sandford Fleming. Use a dictionary if necessary.

   conscientious   inventive

   precise   sloppy

3. What does the story say was the effect of Fleming missing his train?

   _____

   _____

4. In the final sentence of this story, what does the word *adopted* mean?

   a. taken into their homes

   b. legally become part of a family

   c. started to use

   d. rejected

5. Use a map or the Internet to learn about time zones. How did Fleming's ideas change the way people tell time today? Write a paragraph on a separate sheet of paper.

Vocabulary

Read the story. Then, answer the questions.

Harriet Tubman

Harriet Tubman was a brave woman. Tubman grew up as a slave in Maryland. She escaped north to Philadelphia, Pennsylvania, as an adult. Tubman returned to Maryland to help rescue her family. She returned again and again to help other slaves. Tubman guided them to safe houses along a network known as the Underground Railroad. People who helped slaves move to safety were called "conductors." These conductors were named after the people who controlled trains on railroads. In 1861, the United States began fighting the Civil War. Part of the struggle between the northern states and the southern states was about whether people should be allowed to own slaves. In 1863, President Abraham Lincoln signed a law stating that slavery was no longer allowed in the United States. With the law on her side, Tubman continued to help people who were treated unfairly. She died in 1913.

1. What is the main idea of this story?

   _____

2. What did people in Tubman's time believe about slavery?

   _____

   _____

3. What does the phrase *Underground Railroad* mean in this story?

   a. a subway system   b. a hidden railway

   c. a secret system of safe houses d. a secret passageway

4. You can tell a lot about people by what they do. Circle the adjective(s) that you think describe Harriet Tubman. Use a dictionary if necessary.

   courageous   meek   resourceful   content

5. Why do you think Tubman kept returning to help other slaves?

   _____

6. Use reference books or the Internet to learn about the Underground Railroad. On a separate sheet of paper, write a paragraph describing the Underground Railroad and how it was used.

Name _____

Vocabulary

Read the story. Then, answer the questions.

Flags of the World

A flag tells something special about a country or a group. Look at the US flag. The 13 stripes are for the first 13 states. The stripes are red and white. The 50 stars are for the current 50 states. The stars are on a blue field. Look at the Canadian flag. It has a red maple leaf on white between two bands of red. The maple leaf stands for the nature found in Canada. Canadian provinces and US states also have their own flags. The state flag of Texas has a large white star on blue on the left and two bands of red and white on the right. Because of the flag's single star, Texas is called the Lone Star State. The flag of the Canadian province of New Brunswick has a gold lion on a red field above a sailing ship. The lion stands for ties to Brunswick, Germany, and the British king. The ship represents the shipping industry. The United Nations is a group of countries that works for world peace. It has a flag too. Its flag shows a globe surrounded by olive leaves, which are a symbol of peace.

1. What is the main idea of this story?

   a. A flag tells something special about a country or group.

   b. Some flags have maple leaves or lions on them.

   c. Many flags are red, white, or blue.

2. Why is Texas called the Lone Star State?

   _____

3. What does the word *field* mean in this story?

   a. an area of grass

   b. a large area of a single color

   c. an area of study

4. Use an encyclopedia or the Internet to look at different countries' flags. On a separate sheet of paper, design a flag to represent your school. Carefully choose colors, shapes, and other symbols. Describe these symbols on a second sheet of paper. Include the reasons for your design.

Vocabulary

Read the story. Then, answer the questions.

City Government

A president is a key national leader. So is a prime minister. Your city also has important leaders. Many cities have a mayor. The mayor goes to events like the opening of a new library or a parade. The mayor often works with the city council. This is a group of people from areas all over the city. They work together to solve problems that will help citizens. A city may also have a manager. The city manager makes sure that city services are running smoothly from day to day. This person also creates a budget. The budget shows how the city should spend its money. There are many other members of city government. They include the chief of police and the fire chief. These people lead the police and fire departments. They make rules that their employees must follow. A city needs many workers to make a better life for everyone.

1. What is the main idea of this story?

   a. The president is an important leader.

   b. The leader of the police is called a chief.

   c. City government includes many different workers.

2. What does a city manager do?

   _____

   _____

3. What is a *budget*?

   a. a report that tells how the city should spend its money

   b. a city manager

   c. a person who leads the fire department

4. Why does a city need many workers?

   _____

5. Think about your school. You and your classmates are citizens. The teachers, custodians, and other staff are workers as well as citizens. On a separate sheet of paper, make a chart showing your school's organization. Start at the top of the page. Draw a circle for the principal. Then, draw other circles for other jobs. Label the circles.

Name _____

Vocabulary

Read the story. Then, answer the questions.

The Olympic Games

People from all over the world take part in the Olympic Games. They gather to compete in different sports. The original Olympics were held in Greece around 776 BCE. They occurred every four years. Young men ran races of different lengths. Winners were given wreaths of olive branches. The modern Olympics resumed in 1896. That year, they were held in Greece. In 1996, people decided to split the Olympic Games. Now, the summer and winter Olympics are held separately. The Olympics now occur every two years. People from more than 200 countries compete in either summer or winter sports. Today's winners receive gold, silver, or bronze medals. They compete in hundreds of events. The Olympics are good for the host countries too. It gives them a chance to show off their culture. Both the people who attend and the people who watch on TV learn about the host country. The sports may differ from the original Olympics, but the spirit of goodwill and good sportsmanship is still the same.

1. What is the main idea of this story?

    a. The Olympics are held every four years.

    b. People come to the Olympics to compete in different sports.

    c. Good sportsmanship is very important at the Olympics.

2. When and where were the first Olympics held?

    _____

3. How do the Olympics help people learn about different cultures?

    _____

4. Two athletes have just won gold and silver at the Olympics. What are they thinking? Write your answer from the point of view of each athlete. Use complete sentences.

    Gold medal winner: _____

    Silver medal winner: _____

5. The author uses the word *culture* in this story. Culture can include a lot of things about a group of people. What does it NOT include?

    a. music   b. language   c. clothing   d. air

6. Make a Venn diagram on a separate sheet of paper. In one circle, write your favorite sport. In the other circle, write another sport. Compare and contrast the differences and similarities between the sports.

Vocabulary

Read the story. Then, answer the questions.

Cleaning Up Earth

We have many cities to live in. But, we have only one Earth. We cannot move to a new one. So, it is important to take care of our planet. You may have heard the phrase "Reduce, reuse, recycle." Putting these words into action will help keep Earth clean. First, reduce the amount of waste you make. Cook with fresh fruits and vegetables instead of packaged foods. Second, reuse things when you can. Don't throw that milk carton in the trash. Make a bird feeder from it instead! Do you have extra clothes? Don't toss them out. Donate them! Finally, recycle plastic, glass, metal cans, and paper. These materials can be turned into new items to sell. Then, they won't clog up a landfill. Practice "reduce, reuse, recycle." If we all work together, Earth will be a cleaner, better place for years to come.

1. What is the main idea of this story?

    a. Keeping Earth clean is important for everyone.

    b. Fresh vegetables taste better than packaged ones.

    c. Earth has too much trash.

2. Describe the differences between *reduce, reuse*, and *recycle*.

    _____

    _____

3. How can you reduce the amount of waste you produce?

    _____

4. Think of new ways to help clean up Earth. Write your ideas in complete sentences on a separate sheet of paper. Try to think of at least three ways each to reduce, reuse, and recycle. Share your work with friends. Try to follow through on at least one of these ideas.

Vocabulary

Read the story. Then, answer the questions.

The Continents

Earth is divided into seven large areas of land. These areas are called continents. The seven continents are Asia, Africa, Australia, Europe, Antarctica, North America, and South America. Each continent is separated from the others by a landform such as an ocean or a mountain range. Continents may be divided into many smaller areas as well. These areas are called countries, states, or provinces. People live on six of the seven continents. The continent of Antarctica is at the South Pole. The weather there is too cold for people to live. Some scientists study at the South Pole at special stations, but many stay there for only part of the year. The largest continent is Asia. Asia covers over 17,000,000 square miles (44,000,000 square km). The smallest is Australia, which covers nearly 3,000,000 square miles (7,700,000 square km). Asia also has the most people. Its population is over three billion. That accounts for about half of the world's people!

1. What is the main idea of this story?

   a. More people live in Asia than on any other continent.

   b. It is hard for people to live in Antarctica.

   c. Continents are large areas of land on Earth.

2. What separates continents from each other?

   _____

3. What is a *station* in the story?

   a. a place where scientists study

   b. an area of the classroom

   c. a TV channel

4. Why do you think so many people live in Asia?

   _____

5. At the top of a separate sheet of paper, write "My Home." Divide the page into two sections. On the left side, start a list by writing the name of the largest place in which you live: Earth. Leave two blank lines below. Then, write the name of the next largest place in which you live: North America. Leave two more blank lines. Continue down the page until you reach the smallest place: your room or home. Use the right side of the page to write two complete descriptive sentences about each place.

Vocabulary
Read the story. Then, answer the questions.

Planning a City

What do the streets in your city look like? Some cities have streets that are very straight and organized. It is easy to get from one point in the city to another. Other cities have streets that seem to go nowhere. It may be difficult to give directions to your home. When a group of people move to a place and start setting up the streets, they may use something called a grid system. One example of this is found in the city of Philadelphia, Pennsylvania, which is divided into four sections around a central square. The map was laid out by William Penn in 1682. The grid included wide streets that were easy for people to walk down. Penn left London, England, after a fire destroyed most of the city. London had a maze of narrow streets that were hard to move around safely. Penn wanted to make sure people could get around the city easily and safely. Many other cities followed Penn's ideas when setting up their street systems.

1. What is the main idea of this story?

   a. William Penn drew the first grid system.

   b. Planning a city is important for safety.

   c. Some streets are straight and organized.

2. What is one good thing about having straight streets?

   _____

3. What is a *grid system*?

   _____

4. Why did Penn leave London?

   _____

5. How are Philadelphia's streets different from London's?

   _____

   _____

6. What kind of street do you live on? Is it busy or quiet? Is it wide or narrow? Is it paved or gravel? Write a paragraph on a separate sheet of paper describing the streets where you live.

Vocabulary

Read the story. Then, answer the questions.

Magnets

A magnet is any object with a magnetic field. This means that it pulls things made of iron, steel, or nickel toward it. If you set a paper clip next to a magnet on a table, the paper clip will move toward the magnet. Every magnet has what is called a north pole and a south pole. The north pole of one magnet will stick to the south pole of another magnet. If you try to push the south poles of two magnets together, they will spring apart. Earth has magnetic poles too. Earth is a big magnet! Earth's magnetic poles are not actual places. They are areas of Earth's magnetic field with a certain property. Although Earth's magnetic poles are different than the poles where polar bears live, its magnetic poles are near these poles. The north pole of a magnet will always try to point toward Earth's north magnetic pole. A compass is a piece of camping equipment that shows direction. It has a magnetized needle. This needle points to Earth's magnetic north pole. So, if you get lost, pull out your compass and set it on a flat surface. Wait for the needle to point north.

1. What is the main idea of this story?
    a. If you get lost in the woods, start walking north.
    b. Compasses work by pointing to the north.
    c. Magnets are objects that have magnetic fields.

2. What happens if you push two south poles together?

_____

3. In the phrase *north pole of a magnet*, what does the word *pole* mean?
    a. the part that is attached to a tall post or tree
    b. the part that will always point toward Earth's north magnetic pole
    c. positive
    d. negative

4. Use an encyclopedia or the Internet to learn about the history of the compass. Compare the first compasses to the compass you would take on a camping trip today. Write your answer in the form of a paragraph on a separate sheet of paper. Use a computer to publish your writing. Share your research.

Vocabulary

Read the story. Then, answer the questions.

Reptiles and Amphibians

You may think that lizards and frogs are in the same family. They are not! They are actually quite different. Lizards, snakes, turtles, and crocodiles are reptiles. Frogs, toads, and salamanders are amphibians. Both amphibians and reptiles are cold-blooded. Cold-blooded animals depend on their surroundings for their body temperature. Most amphibians and reptiles lay eggs instead of giving birth to their young. Reptiles lay hard-shelled eggs in nests. Amphibians lay soft-shelled eggs underwater. When reptiles hatch, they look like tiny adults. Amphibian babies might not. Baby frogs, called tadpoles, have to live underwater until they are older. Reptiles feel dry and scaly to the touch. Amphibians feel moist and sticky. Adult amphibians spend their time both in water and on land. This makes amphibians more at risk for becoming sick from pollution. It is important to keep ponds and lakes clean so that the animals that live there will be safe.

1. What is the main idea of this story?

    a. There are important differences between reptiles and amphibians.

    b. Reptiles are the same as amphibians.

    c. Frogs and lizards belong to different families.

2. How are amphibians and reptiles similar?

    _____

    _____

3. Why is it important to keep ponds and lakes clean?

    _____

    _____

4. Reread the first sentence of this story. What is another word or phrase with the same meaning as *family*?

    a. related siblings

    b. geckos and toads

    c. parents or grandparents

    d. related species

5. Choose one amphibian and one reptile. Use an encyclopedia or the Internet to learn about these animals. Use your research to compare them. Write a paragraph on a separate sheet of paper. Use a computer to publish your writing. Share your research.

Vocabulary

Read the story. Then, answer the questions.

Solid, Liquid, Gas

All matter on Earth exists in one of three states: solid, liquid, or gas. Solids, such as boxes or books, have a certain shape that is hard to change. Liquids, such as lemonade or orange juice, take the shape of the bottle or cup they are in. Gases, such as the air you breathe, spread out to fill the space they are in. It is easy to change water from one state to another. The water that you drink is a liquid. When water is heated, such as in a pot on the stove, it becomes a gas. This gas is known as steam, or vapor. Steam is used in an iron to make clothes smooth. It also can be used in a large machine to make electricity. When water is frozen, such as in a tray in the freezer, it turns into ice. Ice is used to cool down drinks or to help a hurt part of the body heal.

1. What is the main idea of this story?

    a. Steam is heated water.

    b. All matter exists as a solid, liquid, or gas.

    c. Ice cubes make water taste better.

2. What do you call water in the three states of matter?

    _____

Are the following sentences true or false? Write **T** or **F**.

3. _____ Lemonade is a solid that takes the shape of its container.

4. _____ Your body is composed of solids, liquids, and gases.

5. Reread the first sentence of this story. What is another word or phrase with the same meaning as *states*?

    a. groups arranged by similarities

    b. provinces or countries

    c. groups arranged by nationality

    d. to say or announce

6. Think of three things: one solid, one liquid, and one gas. Use your personal experience or the Internet to learn about these objects. Use your research to compare them. Think about how these things are used. Although they exist in different states, are there any similarities? Organize your research in the form of three paragraphs on a separate sheet of paper. Use a computer to publish your writing.

Point of View

Read the story. Then, answer the questions.

Computers

Have you ever used a computer at school, at the library, or at home? Today's computers can fit on a desktop or in your lap. Computers of the past took up a whole room! One of the first computers was called the ENIAC, which stood for Electronic Numerical Integrator and Calculator. It took up 1,800 square feet (167 square m), weighed nearly 50 tons, and cost $500,000. The ENIAC took three years to build and was designed for the US Army. It required a team of six people to program it, or tell it what to do. The ENIAC was used from 1947 to 1955. In contrast, a personal computer today can weigh as little as two pounds (1 kg) and can be operated by one person at a time. The builders of the ENIAC may never have believed students could do their homework on computers.

1. What is the main idea of this story?

   a. The ENIAC was an early computer.

   b. Computers of the past were very different from the ones today.

   c. Students can do their homework on computers.

2. What does the word *program* mean in this story?

   a. build a computer

   b. require six people to use

   c. tell a computer what to do

3. How are computers today different from those of the past?

   _____

   _____

4. How is your point of view about computers different from the author's view?

   _____

   _____

Point of View

Read the story. Then, answer the questions.

Food Webs

A food web is a drawing that shows how different living things are connected. On the web drawing, it shows which animals at the top eat the animals directly below them, and so on, until the bottom of the web. For example, a food web might start at the bottom with plants like grass and nuts, which do not eat other living things. Above these plants might be small animals such as mice and insects. Larger animals like owls and snakes eat the smaller animals. A food web can tell you what might happen if different plants or animals disappear from an ecosystem, or the surroundings in which all of these things live. In the food web described above, if something happened to the grass, then the mice and insects would not have much food. This would affect the owls and snakes, which would also not have enough food. Soon, there would be fewer of every animal. This is why it is important to protect all living things in an ecosystem, not just the largest ones.

1. What is the main idea of this story?

    a. Food webs show how all living things are connected.

    b. Owls and snakes are the most important animals.

    c. Only the animals at the top should be protected.

2. What is an *ecosystem*?

    a. a food web for very large animals

    b. the surroundings where a group of plants and animals live

    c. a place that grows only grass and nuts

3. A food web is a cause-and-effect chain. In this story, what might contribute to, or cause, a decrease in the owl population?

    _____

4. Answer the following question in complete sentences, written from each animal's point of view.

    How does the food web affect my life?

    Mouse: _____

    Snake: _____

5. Write the name of a small plant or insect at the bottom of a separate sheet of paper. Use research from an encyclopedia or the Internet to draw a food web, starting from this plant or insect. Continue up the food web as many levels as possible. Display your food web in your classroom and discuss your findings.

Point of View

Read the story. Then, answer the questions.

Floods

Rain is good for people and plants. We need rain. But, when it rains too much, people may be in danger. Flash floods are dangerous. They occur when a lot of rain falls very quickly. The rain fills the streets faster than the water can drain away. It is very risky to drive in a flash flood. Your car may be swept away. If you live in an area where flooding is likely, listen to the radio or TV when it starts to rain. A newscaster may tell you to move to a higher location. Be ready to leave your home. Before you leave, turn off all electrical equipment. Move important items to a higher floor, if possible. If you leave on foot, do not walk through moving water. Do not drive through standing water unless it is less than six inches (15.24 cm) deep. After a flood, listen to news reports again. The newscaster will tell you when you can return home and when the water from your tap will be safe to drink.

1. What is the main idea of this story?

   a. Flash floods can be dangerous and happen suddenly.

   b. Never drive through a flooded area.

   c. Take important items with you when you leave your home.

2. When should you leave your home?

   _____

3. What should you do before leaving your home?

   _____

   _____

4. What might contribute to, or cause, a car to be swept away? Write your answer in a complete sentence.

   _____

5. What does the phrase *standing water* mean in this story:

   a. water with feet   b. flowing water   c. still water   d. drinkable water

6. How does the author feel about rain? Is this the same as or different from your point of view about rain? On a separate sheet of paper, write a paragraph explaining your point of view.

Point of View

Read the story. Then, answer the questions.

Silkworms

Silk is a soft, smooth type of cloth that is used for clothing, bedding, and wall hangings. It comes from silkworm cocoons, which are spun into thread that is then made into cloth. It takes about 3,000 cocoons to make one pound (about 0.5 kg) of silk. Silkworms become moths as adults. Like most insects, silkworms go through four stages. The moth lays its eggs on a mulberry leaf. After a silkworm hatches into a caterpillar, it munches on leaves until it grows to about the length of a human finger. After about a month of eating and growing, the worm spins a cocoon of silk around itself. Spinning the cocoon takes about three days. Inside the cocoon, the silkworm changes shape and becomes a pupa. After about three weeks, the pupa turns into a moth. The moth comes out of the cocoon and starts the cycle all over again.

1. What is the main idea of this story?

   a. Silkworm cocoons are spun into thread.

   b. Silkworms turn into moths as adults.

   c. Silkworms go through four stages and help make silk.

2. What are the stages of a silkworm's life?

   _____

3. The word *stage* can have several meanings. Which sentence uses *stage* in the same way as the author of this story?

   a. The school auditorium has a huge stage.

   b. The actors will stage a play in December.

   c. My baby sister is at a crawling stage.

   d. My friend likes to dance on the stage.

4. Use an encyclopedia or the Internet to learn more about the silkworm. Write a description of the silkworm's life cycle from its point of view. Use a computer to publish your writing.

Point of View

Read the story. Then, answer the questions.

Science Experiments

Scientists learn about the world by conducting experiments. They take careful notes on the supplies they use and the results they find. They share their findings with others. This leads to everyone learning a little more. You can do experiments too! The library has many books with safe experiments for students. You might work with balloons, water, or baking soda. You might learn about how light travels. You might find out why marbles roll down a ramp. Ask an adult to help you set up your experiment. Let him watch to make sure you are being safe. Be sure to wash your hands afterward. And, remember to clean up the area. Take good notes on your work. You may be able to change just one thing the next time. This might give you a completely different result. Do not worry if your results are not what you expected. Some of the greatest scientific discoveries were made by mistake!

1. What is the main idea of this story?

    a. Students can do experiments too, as long as they are safe.

    b. Scientists often make mistakes that lead to great discoveries.

    c. You should always take good notes when conducting an experiment.

2. Where can you find information about safe experiments?

    _____

3. Should you worry if you get different results? Why or why not?

    _____

    _____

4. Which sentence(s) do you think a good scientist would NOT say?

    a. "I don't have to write that down. I'm sure I will remember it."

    b. "I should double-check my measurements."

    c. "I'm not going to bother to measure this water."

    d. "It worked once, so I don't have to do it again."

5. What is the author's point of view about science experiments? How do you know? Explain your answer on a separate sheet of paper.

Point of View

Read the story. Then, answer the questions.

Glaciers

A glacier is a large, thick mass of ice. It forms when snow hardens into ice over a long period of time. It might not look like it, but glaciers can move. They usually move very slowly. However, if a lot of the ice melts at once, the glacier may surge forward, or move suddenly over a long distance. Most glaciers are found in Antarctica, the continent at the South Pole, or in Greenland, which is near the North Pole. Areas with glaciers receive a lot of snowfall in the winter. These areas also have cool summers. Most glaciers are located in the mountains where few people live. Sometimes, the glaciers can cause flooding in cities and towns. Falling ice from glaciers may block hiking trails farther down on the mountains. Icebergs are large floating pieces of ice. Icebergs may break off from glaciers and cause problems for ships at sea.

1. What is the main idea of this story?

    a. Icebergs can be dangerous to ships.

    b. Glaciers are large masses of ice found mainly in the mountains.

    c. People usually live far from glaciers.

2. Where are most glaciers found?

    _____

3. What is the weather like where glaciers are found?

    _____

4. How can glaciers be dangerous?

    _____

5. The word *surge* means to flow in waves or bursts. Which sentence does not use *surge* correctly?

    a. The sudden surge of electricity caused the power to go out.

    b. The library flooded in that storm surge.

    c. He surged forward on the last lap and won the race.

    d. The clock surged in a regular tick-tock rhythm.

6. How do you feel about glaciers after reading this story? Did the author's point of view change your opinion? Why or why not? Explain your answer on a separate sheet of paper.

Visual Aids

Read the story. Then, answer the questions.

Tornadoes

A tornado is a funnel cloud that forms over land. It is created when warm air meets cold air. This makes a thunderstorm. Tornadoes can be very dangerous to both people and things. They can leave a trail of damage one mile (1.6 km) wide and 50 miles (80 km) long. The wind speed can reach over 300 miles (480 km) per hour. People often have little warning of a tornado, but certain parts of the United States have tornadoes more often than other parts. One area is called "Tornado Alley." It includes parts of Texas, Oklahoma, Kansas, Nebraska, Iowa, and South Dakota. Tornadoes are more likely to form in the spring and summer. If a weather reporter says that a tornado has been spotted in your area, stay inside. Go to the lowest level of your home. Keep as many walls as possible between you and the outside. Keep the windows closed. Do not leave until you hear that the tornado has passed.

1. What is the main idea of this story?

   a. Tornadoes are formed during thunderstorms.

   b. Tornado Alley is an area where many storms occur.

   c. Tornadoes are dangerous to people and things.

2. When are tornadoes more likely to form?

   _____

3. What illustrations (e.g., diagrams, photographs) would help you understand this story better? How?

   _____

   _____

4. Pretend you are a weather reporter. You must warn your listeners about a tornado. You need to report the tornado's movements and remind people how to protect themselves. Write your report on a separate sheet of paper. Use a dictionary or a thesaurus to help make your report more dramatic. Then, read your report aloud to your class.

Visual Aids

Read the story. Then, answer the questions.

Sea Urchins

Sea urchins look like pincushions that live under the sea. They have long, thin spines that stick out all over their bodies. Most sea urchins have spines that are about 0.39 to 1.18 inches (1 to 3 cm) long. Sea urchins are found in oceans all over the world. They can be many colors, from green to brown to red. Their bodies are about 4 inches (10 cm) across. They eat dead fish, seaweed, and very tiny plants called algae. Their spines help them trap food. They also use their five tiny teeth to pull plants off rocks. Hundreds of tiny tubes used as feet help them move along the seafloor. Many creatures, including sea otters, crabs, and eels, like to eat sea urchins.

1. What is the main idea of this story?

    a. Sea urchins are interesting animals that live in the ocean.

    b. Sea urchins taste salty and creamy.

    c. Sea urchins look like pincushions.

2. How do sea urchins move?

    _____

3. How do sea urchins pull plants off rocks?

    _____

4. What illustration (e.g., diagrams, photographs) would help you understand this story better? How?

    _____

    _____

5. Pretend you are a spokesperson for an aquarium. You want people to come see all of the animals, not just the dolphins and penguins. On another sheet of paper, create an advertisement that will persuade people to visit the sea urchins. Use an encyclopedia or the Internet to discover more interesting facts. Share your ad with your class.

Visual Aids

Read the story. Then, answer the questions.

Health and Fitness

Health and fitness are very important for young people. If you start good habits now, you have a better chance of being a healthy adult later. You may go to gym class several times a week, but you should also try to stay fit outside of school. You and your family can make healthy choices together. You can choose fresh fruit for dessert instead of cake. Offer to help make dinner one night and surprise your family by preparing a delicious salad. You can go for a walk together after dinner instead of watching TV. Exercising can help wake up your brain so that you can do a good job on your homework. Making healthy choices may seem hard now, but after a while, it will feel good.

1. What is the main idea of this story?

   a. Going to gym class is fun.

   b. Making healthy choices is too hard.

   c. Health and fitness are important for you and your family.

2. Where should you try to stay fit?

   _____

3. How does exercise affect your brain?

   _____

4. What does this story say may contribute to becoming a healthy adult?

   _____

5. The word *fit* has several meanings. Which one of these sentences uses *fit* in the same way as in the story?

   a. The house is a good fit for Grandpa because it is close to the golf course.

   b. We had to bring our dog to the vet because he was having a fit.

   c. That marathon runner must really be fit!

   d. The plumber fit the new piece onto the pipe.

6. Would illustrations (e.g., diagrams, photographs) help you understand this story better? Why or why not? Explain your answer on a separate sheet of paper.

Name _____

3.W.1, 3.L.2, 3.L.6

Opinion Writing

Look at the list of words below. Write each word in the correct category.

Sports

bases	goalie	mound	pool
dive	goggles	pass	score
glove	kick	pitcher	swimsuit

Swimming   **Soccer**   **Baseball**

_____   _____   _____

_____   _____   _____

_____   _____   _____

_____   _____   _____

Imagine a coach has asked if you are interested in participating in one of the sports listed above. On a separate sheet of paper, answer in the form of a letter written to the coach. Explain why you do or do not want to participate in that sport. Use at least three words from the list in your letter. Your letter should contain at least four complete sentences.

© Carson-Dellosa • CD-104621

Opinion Writing

Look at the list of words below. Write each word in the correct category.

Weather

blazing	mittens	splash	thunder
hot	puddle	summer	umbrella
icy	shovel	swimming	winter

Sunny   **Snowy**   **Rainy**

_____   _____   _____

_____   _____   _____

_____   _____   _____

_____   _____   _____

What type of weather do you like best? On a separate sheet of paper, explain why you like this type of weather. In the second paragraph, explain what you do not like about other types of weather. Use at least six words from the list. Give reasons to support your opinion.

Opinion Writing

Look at the list of words below. Write each word in the correct category.

Senses

barking	eyelid	noise	radio
concert	glasses	perfume	skunk
cookies	lemon	picture	watch

Sight	**Hearing**	**Smell**
_____	_____	_____
_____	_____	_____
_____	_____	_____
_____	_____	_____

On a separate sheet of paper, explain how you use your sense of sight, hearing, and smell. Use at least nine words from the list. In your conclusion, state which sense you believe people use the most. Give reasons to support your opinion.

Informative Writing

Look at the list of words below. Write each word in the correct category.

Animals

elephant	hamster	lion	rabbit
giraffe	kangaroo	penguin	turtle
goldfish	kitten	puppy	zebra

Pets   **Zoo Animals**

_____   _____   _____   _____

_____   _____   _____   _____

_____   _____   _____   _____

Choose an animal from the lists. Use an encyclopedia or the Internet to research more about this animal. On a separate sheet of paper, write a short paragraph describing your animal. Add illustrations to make your description clearer.

Informative Writing

Look at the list of words below. Write each word in the correct category .

Food

cereal	fruit	peas	salad
dumplings	juice	pizza	sausage
fish	pancakes	rice	toast

Breakfast   **Dinner**

_____   _____   _____   _____

_____   _____   _____   _____

_____   _____   _____   _____

On a separate sheet of paper, describe what you might eat for breakfast and dinner. Organize your work into two short paragraphs, one for each meal. Use at least six words from the list. Add illustrations to make your description clearer.

Informative Writing

Look at the list of words below. Write each word in the correct category.

Rooms

apron	dishwasher	hangers	stove
blanket	flour	pajamas	teapot
clothes	fork	slippers	toys

Bedroom   **Kitchen**

_____   _____   _____   _____

_____   _____   _____   _____

_____   _____   _____   _____

On a separate sheet of paper, describe a bedroom and kitchen. Organize your work into two paragraphs. Use at least nine words from the list. Add illustrations to make your descriptions clearer.

Narrative Writing

Look at the list of words below. Write each word in the correct category.

Time

awake	daylight	moonlight	sleep
bedtime	dusk	noon	sunlight
dawn	midnight	school	sunset

Day   **Night**

_____ _____   _____ _____

_____ _____   _____ _____

_____ _____   _____ _____

Pretend you are an imaginary character, such as a pirate, an elf, or a unicorn. Write a short story from your new point of view to describe a day (or a night) in your life. Include at least three words from the list. Use dialogue to help describe your feelings and thoughts. After revising, read your story aloud to your family or friends.

Narrative Writing

Look at the list of words below. Write each word in the correct category.

Extreme Places

anchor	camel	sandstorm	thirsty
beach	lighthouse	scorpions	tide
cactus	oasis	seagulls	waves

Ocean   **Desert**

_____ _____   _____ _____

_____ _____   _____ _____

_____ _____   _____ _____

Imagine being lost at sea in a small boat or wandering through a desert on foot. Write a short story to describe your adventure. Your story should include at least four words from the list. Use dialogue to help describe your feelings and thoughts. After revising, read your story aloud to your family or friends.

Narrative Writing

Look at the list of words below. Write each word in the correct category.

Dream Vacation

astronaut	comet	gravity	peak
avalanche	climb	orbit	spacesuit
cold	galaxy	oxygen	towering

Visiting the Moon   **Climbing Mount Everest**

_____ _____   _____ _____

_____ _____   _____ _____

_____ _____   _____ _____

Imagine your Uncle Pete has invited you on vacation. You can blast to the moon, or you can climb the tallest mountain in the world. Your only human companion will be Uncle Pete. Write a short story to describe your adventure. Your story should include at least five words from the list. Describe actions and events as they happen. Use dialogue to help describe your feelings and thoughts. After revising, read your story aloud to your family or friends.

Word Endings

Fill in each blank with the word that makes the most sense in the sentence.

hay	may	ray	tray

1. Mom, _____ I have some more grapes, please?

2. Horses like to eat _____ .

3. Please take the _____ of food to your table.

4. A _____ of light shined on my pillow.

splash	dash	flash	mash

5. Bill likes to _____ in the water.

6. A _____ of lightning lit the sky.

7. Jill won the 50-yard _____ .

8. Dad will _____ potatoes for dinner.

sped	led	bred	fled

9. The lion almost caught the gazelles before they _____ .

10. Carlos _____ during most of the race, but Jayla won.

11. Some kinds of dogs are _____ to fetch things.

12. The police car _____ to the accident.

Word Endings

Fill in each blank with a word from the *-ight* family that makes the most sense in the sentence.

1. We took a _____ on an airplane to see Grandma.

2. Casey's old shoes are too _____ to wear.

3. Our eyes give us the sense of _____ .

4. Hilda shined the _____ flashlight on the ground.

5. The empty box was very _____ to carry.

Fill in each blank with a word from the *-ive* family that makes the most sense in the sentence.

6. What time should we _____ for the party?

7. Zach and Katie saw their favorite singer _____ in concert.

8. The human body has _____ senses.

9. The bees buzzed around their _____ .

10. Aunt Sharon will _____ us to the game.

Fill in each blank with a word from the *-aw* family that makes the most sense in the sentence.

11. The ice will _____ if it gets warm outside.

12. The teacher will _____ the winner's name out of a hat.

13. Do not break the _____ by speeding!

14. Beavers like to _____ on trees with their big front teeth.

15. When they _____ the new puppy, they wanted to keep it.

Word Endings

Fill in each blank with the word that makes the most sense in the sentence. It may be helpful to cross off the words in the word bank as you use them.

clip	drip	flip	sip	snip	trip

1. My dad can _____ the pancakes in the pan.

2. Melting ice will _____ in your hand.

3. Julio will _____ the papers together.

4. The kitten likes to _____ milk.

5. Jessica used scissors to _____ the thread.

6. I am going on a _____ to see Grandpa.

crop	drop	flop	mop	pop	stop

7. When I am tired, I _____ onto my bed and rest.

8. I _____ at the crosswalk and look both ways.

9. A _____ of water fell into the sink.

10. The farmer planted his _____ of wheat.

11. Liv needed to _____ up the spill.

12. Please do not _____ my balloon.

Word Endings

Fill in each blank with the word that makes the most sense in the sentence.

cream	dream	gleam	steam

1. The boiling water turned into _____ .

2. My teeth always _____ after I visit the dentist.

3. Juan's _____ is to become a teacher.

4. We had ice _____ with our cake.

bow	cow	plow	how

5. The farmer had to _____ the field.

6. This milk comes from a _____ .

7. The actors took a _____ .

8. George showed me _____ to boil eggs.

brain	gain	grain	pain

9. When my arm broke, I was in _____ .

10. Bread is made from _____ .

11. I use my _____ to spell words.

12. As the puppy eats more, he will _____ weight.

Word Endings

Fill in each blank with a word from the -ace family that makes the most sense in the sentence.

1. Mei walked away at a quick _____ .

2. Someday, I want to go to outer _____ .

3. At bedtime, you should wash your _____ .

4. Go back to the _____ you started.

5. Angelo did not leave a _____ of food on his plate.

Fill in each blank with a word from the -are family that makes the most sense in the sentence.

6. We paid our _____ on the train.

7. A _____ is like a rabbit.

8. Don't you _____ touch that stove!

9. Please keep your _____ feet off the furniture.

10. A female horse is called a _____ .

Fill in each blank with a word from the -out family that makes the most sense in the sentence.

11. I heard someone _____, "Fire! Fire!"

12. Gavin placed the water pail under the _____ and began to pump.

13. I think the rainbow _____ is the most beautiful fish in the world.

14. We will learn _____ caterpillars today.

15. A pig's _____ is round and flat.

Compound Words

A compound word is two words that have been put together to make a new word. For example, *thumb* and *print* can be put together to make the new word *thumbprint*. Look at each list of compound words. Fill in each blank in the stories below with the best compound word. Use each word once. Use captial letters when necessary.

| necktie | earrings | briefcases | everyone |
| raincoats | necklace | stepmother | shoelaces |

Getting Ready for the Day

_____ in my family gets ready for the day in a different way. My _____

puts on her jewelry like her _____ and a _____ . Dad puts on a

_____ . They both pick up their _____ to take to work. I just tie my

_____ , and I am ready to go! When the weather is bad, we all do one thing the same.

We all put on our _____ .

| suitcases | takeoff | doorway | headphones |
| airport | gumball | headband | airplane |

Flying

Last year, Mom and I flew to visit Grandpa. We got to the _____ early and put tags

on our _____ . When the _____ arrived, we got in line to board. We

walked through the _____ of the airplane and found our seats. I took off my

_____ , and Mom gave me some _____ so that I could listen to music.

After _____ , my ears hurt a little, so Mom gave me a _____ to chew.

Name _____

Compound Words

Look at each list of compound words. Fill in each blank in the stories below with the best compound word. Use capital letters when necessary. Not all of the words will be used.

| butterflies | rosebush | backyard | fireflies | everywhere | flytrap |
| earthworms | stinkbug | ladybugs | honeybees | rainstorm | beeline |

Insects

Bugs are _____ you look. _____ like to get pollen from flowers.

_____ have colorful wings. _____ are red with black spots.

_____ live in the ground and come out after a _____ . When it is dark,

_____ come out and fly around. It is fun to see them light up in the _____ .

| underwater | catfish | castoff | rowboat | something | shoreline |
| fishhook | campfire | dockyard | sunshine | waterproof | shipwreck |

Fishing

My uncle likes to go fishing. He puts on old clothes and _____ boots and

stands by the water. Sometimes, he goes out in a _____ . He puts bait on a

_____ and throws out the line. The hook sinks _____ . He waits for a

_____ to take the bait. He stands in the _____ and fishes until he

catches _____ . Then, he cooks the fish over a _____ .

Compound Words

Look at each list of words. Fill in each blank in the stories below with the best compound word that you can create from the list. Use each word once.

beat	cakes	fish	grand	pan	summer	time	up
bed	every	gold	mother	room	thing	tub	wash

My Grandmother

I like it when my _____ comes to stay with me in the _____ She is an

_____ person. She knows how to make _____ fun. She tells me stories while

we make _____ in the morning. We splash each other when she shows me how to wash

clothes in a _____ . She sings funny songs while we feed my _____ .

Grandmother even knows games that make _____ fun!

ball	foot	head	knee	off	pads	some	times
down	gear	kick	news	over	paper	time	touch

Football

My brother is on the _____ team. He wears special _____ and

_____ to keep his body safe. I go to watch his games _____ . It is fun to

watch the _____ at the beginning of the game. One day, the game went into

_____ , and they had to play longer. My brother scored the winning _____ !

The next day, his picture was in the _____ !

Name _____

Compound Words

A compound word is two words that have been put together to make a new word. For example, *eye* and *lid* can be put together to make the new word *eyelid*. Look at each list of compound words. Fill in each blank in the stories below with the best compound word. Use each word once.

rainstorms	forecast	snowstorms	snowmen
rainwater	snowflakes	rainfall	thunderclouds

Rain and Snow

The weather _____ tells us what weather we can expect. In the spring, we usually

have _____ with a lot of dark _____ . Our garden needs the

_____ , and we like to collect _____ to water our plants with later. During

winter, we usually get _____ ! We watch the white _____ fall. Later, we go

outside and play in the snow. We even make _____ !

someday	schoolteacher	anything	lawmaker
shoemaker	firefighter	hairdresser	salesperson

Jobs

What job would you like to have _____ when you are an adult? A _____

makes and fixes shoes. A _____ works with children. A _____ cuts people's

hair. Both a police officer and a _____ help people. A _____ sells things.

A _____ works in an office. You can be _____ you choose!

Compound Words

Look at each list of compound words. Fill in each blank in the stories below with the best compound word. Not all of the words will be used.

classroom	lunchtime	seesaw	breakfast	popcorn	hallway
friendship	backpack	paperweight	bookmark	homework	playground

My School Day

Mom wakes me up to get dressed and eat _____ . I pack my _____ and

go to school. I work at my desk in the _____ . When it is _____ , I sit with

my friends. At recess, we go to the _____ . We like to play on the _____ .

At the end of the day, our teacher writes our _____ on the board. After school, I like to

eat _____ for a snack.

nighttime	outside	ballgame	dogwood	nutshells	butterfly
bluebird	lunchtime	backyard	doghouse	playmate	weekend

Weekend Fun

I like the _____ because I get to spend time _____ with my dog Rusty.

In the morning, Rusty comes out of his _____ to play. We play in the _____

until _____ . Rusty likes to bark at the _____ that lives in the garden. He also

likes to chew on the _____ that squirrels have dropped from the trees. When

_____ comes, Rusty and I are ready to sleep!

Compound Words

Look at each list of compound words. Fill in each blank in the stories below with the best compound word that you can create from the list. Use each word once.

bugs	cloth	grass	hoppers	lunch	out	sun	time
burgers	glasses	ham	lady	melon	side	table	water

Picnic

My family loves to go _____ and have a picnic. We spread out the _____

on the ground. At _____ , Grandpa serves us _____ . We eat

_____ for dessert. We watch the green _____ and spotted

_____ move through the grass. I put on my _____ and play with my

cousins.

after	board	box	cup	nap	oat	play	story
bee	book	bumble	meal	noon	pen	sand	time

My Little Sister

My little sister is fun to take care of. She likes to eat _____ for breakfast. In the

_____ , she likes to play in her _____ outside. She gets tired and comes in

for _____ . I take a _____ out of the _____ and read to her.

Her favorite story is about a _____ . After the story, she goes to sleep in her

_____ .

Homophones

Homophones are words that sound alike but are spelled differently. The words also mean different things.

Choose the correct homophone for each sentence.

| course | coarse | groan | grown |

1. My uncle's beard is very _____ .

2. When I am fully _____ , I want to be a nurse.

3. The pain in my leg made me _____ .

4. Of _____ you may have more soup!

| stare | stair | read | red |

5. I sat on the bottom _____ in front of the building.

6. Our teacher _____ a story to us after lunch.

7. My cat likes to _____ out the window.

8. Ling wore a bright _____ dress in the play.

Homophones

Choose the correct homophone for each sentence.

one	won	here	hear	hire	higher

1. We are _____ to learn.

2. My brother hopes they _____ him for the job.

3. David had _____ sticker left, and he gave it to his friend.

4. The airplane flew _____ than the kite.

5. Do you _____ a band playing music?

6. Chang ran fast and _____ the race.

know	no	meet	meat	pause	paws

7. My cat washes her face using her _____ .

8. Maria added _____ to the taco.

9. Did you _____ that ice is frozen water?

10. The students will _____ after school to play games.

11. Please _____ so that I do not miss anything.

12. There are _____ apples left on the tree.

3.RL.4, 3.RF.3, 3.L.4

Homophones

Choose the correct homophone for each sentence.

due	dew	seas	pair	pear	reign
do	seize	sees	pare	rain	rein

1. The fisherman sailed the seven _____ .

2. A fun thing to _____ is visit the creek.

3. Samia's library book is _____ on Monday.

4. Josh _____ his grandparents every weekend.

5. When you _____ something, you grab it.

6. We smelled the morning _____ in the air.

7. The king will _____ for his whole life.

8. When you have a _____ of something, you have two of them.

9. The cool _____ felt good on our hot faces.

10. To make the horse slow down, pull on the _____ .

11. Would you like an apple or a _____ ?

12. Mom will _____ the potatoes before cooking them.

Homophones

> **Homophones** are words that sound alike but are spelled differently. The words also mean different things.

Choose the correct homophone for each sentence.

bury	berry	hare	hair

1. Mom put a fresh _____ in each glass of lemonade.

2. In the story, the fox and the _____ had a race.

3. Our dog likes to _____ the bones we give him.

4. Mark's sister has long brown _____ .

main	mane	wrap	rap

5. The horse's _____ was hard to brush.

6. Please _____ the gift in pretty paper.

7. We heard a _____ at the door.

8. Dave lives on the _____ road in his town.

Homophones

Choose the correct homophone for each sentence.

| right | write | sail | sale | root | route |

1. The _____ of a tooth is below the gum.

2. Mark the _____ answer on your paper.

3. Captain Jung will _____ the boat to shore.

4. The sign says that the car is for _____ .

5. Lillie liked taking the faster _____ to school.

6. I will _____ a story about my town.

| our | hour | side | sighed | weather | whether |

7. We will be home in an _____ .

8. The _____ is beautiful today!

9. Taylor _____ when she sat in her chair.

10. My family loves _____ house.

11. Sierra painted one _____ of the fence purple.

12. Harry wondered _____ he should take an umbrella.

Homophones

Choose the correct homophone for each sentence.

| too | to | scent | new | gnu | rowed |
| two | cent | sent | knew | road | rode |

1. The _____ kittens played with the ball of yarn.

2. A penny equals one _____ .

3. My aunt asked me to go _____ the store.

4. Malcolm _____ a letter to his friend.

5. I will clean my desk and the table _____ .

6. The flower has a sweet _____ .

7. When I saw the lights were off, I _____ no one was home.

8. The wildebeest, also called a _____ , is a type of African antelope.

9. They _____ a boat across the river during the flood.

10. Turn left when you reach the fork in the _____ .

11. We _____ our horses all the way to the ranch.

12. His favorite present was his _____ bicycle.

Homophones

Homophones are words that sound alike but are spelled differently. The words also mean different things.

Choose the correct homophone for each sentence.

beach	beech	hoarse	horse

1. I think I am getting a cold because my voice is _____ .

2. Grandpa had to cut down both the elm tree and the _____ tree.

3. My _____ loves to gallop.

4. My feet are sandy after playing at the _____ .

roll	role	I	eye

5. My friend and _____ ate lunch together.

6. Would you like some butter on your _____ ?

7. Janna played the _____ of the queen.

8. The actor wore a patch over one _____ .

Homophones

Choose the correct homophone for each sentence.

| bare | bear | heel | heal | tale | tail |

1. Joey hurt the _____ of his foot when he stepped on a stone.

2. My favorite _____ is the story about Jack and the giant.

3. A _____ lives in the woods and likes to eat honey.

4. Doctors try to _____ people.

5. Kenan stuck his _____ feet in the swimming pool.

6. Her dog wags his _____ when he is happy.

| fair | fare | maid | made | weak | week |

7. My family went to the state _____ .

8. What is your favorite day of the _____ ?

9. A _____ is someone who helps with cleaning.

10. After Uma won the race, her legs felt _____ .

11. The bus _____ is one dollar.

12. Kim _____ a picture frame for her stepfaher.

Homophones

Choose the correct homophone for each sentence.

or	oar	vein	not	naught	teas
ore	vane	vain	knot	tees	tease

1. It was hard to row the boat with only one _____ .

2. I think Nadia is _____ because she is always looking at herself in the mirror.

3. A weather _____ points in the direction the wind is blowing.

4. Dad was not sure if Teddy _____ I scored that goal.

5. When you give blood, the nurse will put a needle in your _____ .

6. Miners dig for _____ because it is a valuable rock that contains metal.

7. I told you, I am _____ going to leave you behind!

8. My brother likes to _____ me, even though I do not like it.

9. Tito stopped to untie the _____ in his shoelace.

10. Hot black and green _____ are very popular to drink.

11. Another word for *zero* is the word _____ , which means nothing.

12. My dad must have at least a hundred _____ in his golf bag!

Context Clues

When you come to a word and you do not know the meaning, use **context clues** to help you figure it out. Context clues are the words around the word you do not know.

Use context clues to figure out the meaning of each underlined word below. Circle the correct meaning. Use a dictionary to help as needed.

1. My style is to wear T-shirts and jeans, but my sister wears fancy dresses.
    a. clothes
    b. fashion
    c. boots

2. I avoid eating snacks before dinnertime.
    a. stay away from
    b. love
    c. try to have

3. Lucy's family permits her to walk home with a friend.
    a. bans
    b. drives
    c. allows

4. The journey from my house to Grandma's takes five hours.
    a. trip
    b. airplane
    c. car

5. My brother built a model airplane. Then, he painted it red and blue.
    a. real
    b. person who shows off clothes
    c. small copy

6. Everyone loves her friendliness and charm.
    a. voice
    b. nice manner
    c. necklace

7. Please notify the coach today if you would like to try out for the team.
    a. tell
    b. obey
    c. play for

Name _____

Context Clues

> Remember, use context clues to figure out the meaning of unknown words.

Use context clues to figure out the meaning of each underlined word below. Circle the correct meaning. Use a dictionary to help as needed.

1. The car tire scraped the <u>curb</u> as it went around the corner.
   a. edge of a road   b. sidewalk   c. boots

2. We went on a <u>march</u> through the neighborhood.
   a. month   b. band   c. walk

3. After Jaden ate the <u>entire</u> pizza, his stomach hurt.
   a. whole   b. wheel   c. small

4. Polar bears live in <u>arctic</u> weather.
   a. very hot   b. rainy   c. very cold

5. My stepmother is helping me study so I can <u>improve</u> my grades.
   a. study   b. raise   c. read

6. My teacher invites families to <u>observe</u> her class so that they know how she teaches.
   a. watch   b. leave   c. teach

7. The <u>motion</u> of the rocking boat made me feel ill.
   a. ocean   b. captain   c. movement

8. The motor is at the <u>rear</u> of the boat, just behind the seats.
   a. side   b. back   c. middle

Context Clues

Use context clues to figure out the meaning of each underlined word below. Circle the correct meaning.
Use a dictionary to help as needed.

1. The <u>principal</u> reason for studying is to learn new things.

   a. main   b. school   c. last

2. The teacher will <u>accept</u> our homework until tomorrow morning.

   a. stay away from   b. give away   c. take

3. We tried all morning, but it was <u>impossible</u> to get tickets to the game.

   a. certain   b. easy   c. not possible

4. Mr. Lee told us the good news with a <u>grin</u> on his face.

   a. cheerful   b. smile   c. sad

5. Jay placed the photograph in a silver <u>frame</u>.

   a. picture holder   b. question   c. snapshot

6. What is your <u>individual</u> opinion about the food?

   a. class   b. own   c. thought

7. My uncle is a soldier in the <u>military</u>.

   a. armed forces   b. officer   c. government

8. Carrie chose the <u>ordinary</u> name Spot for her dalmatian puppy.

   a. unusual   b. normal   c. correct

9. One <u>element</u> of a successful day is getting enough sleep.

   a. start   b. chemical   c. part

Context Clues

> When you come to a word and you do not know the meaning, use **context clues** to help you figure it out. Context clues are the words around the word you do not know.

Use context clues to figure out the meaning of each underlined word below. Circle the correct meaning. Use a dictionary to help as needed.

1. Marcy wanted to <u>magnify</u> the words on the bottle so that she could see them better.
   a. make bigger
   b. copy
   c. read

2. Each person is wearing a <u>label</u> with his or her name on it.
   a. jacket
   b. shirt
   c. tag

3. It is not nice to <u>tease</u> people or animals.
   a. obey
   b. talk to
   c. bother

4. When water is heated, <u>steam</u> rises into the air.
   a. droplets
   b. ice
   c. lakes

5. Mr. Jones <u>conducts</u> the choir when they give a concert.
   a. behavior
   b. leads
   c. does experiments

6. It is always nice to see a <u>familiar</u> face.
   a. unknown
   b. belonging to parents
   c. something that is known

7. Our school's teachers want to <u>educate</u> all of their students.
   a. teach
   b. study
   c. watch

Context Clues

Remember, use context clues to figure out the meaning of unknown words.

Use context clues to figure out the meaning of each underlined word below. Circle the correct meaning. Use a dictionary to help as needed.

1. In North America, people vote to <u>elect</u> their government leaders.

   a. object to   b. choose   c. win

2. The <u>majority</u> of the class voted to have pizza instead of sandwiches for lunch.

   a. most people   b. few people   c. teachers

3. My mom's greatest <u>concern</u> is that we get home safely.

   a. rule   b. problem   c. worry

4. A bride often wears a <u>veil</u> on her head during a wedding.

   a. netting that goes on the head   b. long gown   c. flowers

5. You should always be <u>civil</u> to other students and teachers.

   a. quiet   b. rude   c. polite

6. The new pool is <u>private</u>. Only people who live in that neighborhood can use it.

   a. open   b. not public   c. fun

7. The <u>scent</u> of some flowers makes my nose itch.

   a. sound   b. sight   c. smell

8. I will <u>wrap</u> a gift for Mario to open at his party.

   a. buy   b. speak about   c. put paper around

Context Clues

Use context clues to figure out the meaning of each underlined word below. Circle the correct meaning. Use a dictionary to help as needed.

1. The underwater <u>current</u> can be very strong in the ocean.

   a. breeze   b. beach   c. flow

2. We thought long and hard before making a <u>decision</u>.

   a. argument   b. choice   c. lesson

3. Everyone at the party was very <u>merry</u>.

   a. happy   b. upset   c. small

4. Our teacher will <u>display</u> the class poster for the rest of the school to see.

   a. tear up   b. throw away   c. show

5. After a <u>brief</u> speech from one of the actors, the play began.

   a. quiet   b. short   c. noisy

6. The baby <u>seized</u> the rattle his mom was holding and waved it around.

   a. hit   b. stared at   c. grabbed

7. My cat likes to <u>stare</u> out the window.

   a. watch   b. step   c. bother

8. Mike's dog likes to <u>bury</u> everything in a pile of dirt in the backyard.

   a. eat   b. cover   c. play with

9. It is always best to be <u>honest</u> in what you do and say.

   a. funny   b. truthful   c. sneaky

Context Clues

When you come to a word and you do not know the meaning, use **context clues** to help you figure it out. Context clues are the words around the word you do not know.

Use context clues to figure out the meaning of each underlined word below. Circle the correct meaning. Use a dictionary to help as needed.

1. Before it rains, I can feel the <u>moisture</u> in the air.

   a. thunder   b. sunshine   c. wetness

2. The <u>bark</u> on a tree is very rough.

   a. outer covering   b. leaves   c. sand

3. I <u>groaned</u> when I realized that I had forgotten my book.

   a. shouted   b. whispered   c. sighed loudly

4. My sister <u>beamed</u> when our mother said, "Good job!"

   a. shined a ray of light   b. smiled broadly   c. frowned

5. The <u>fare</u> for riding the train was a dollar for adults.

   a. ticket price   b. store   c. railroad

6. The crowd <u>rumbled</u> like thunder as the news spread.

   a. jumped   b. screamed   c. roared

7. My hand felt <u>weak</u> after I finished writing the report.

   a. strong   b. tired   c. loose

Context Clues

Remember, use context clues to figure out the meaning of unknown words.

Use context clues to figure out the meaning of each underlined word below. Circle the correct meaning. Use a dictionary to help as needed.

1. Dad likes to make a special tomato <u>sauce</u> to put on our pizza.
   a. bowl   b. dinner   c. topping

2. Drop the noodles into the pan when the water starts to <u>boil</u>.
   a. stir   b. heat   c. freeze

3. My mom and stepfather had to sign a special <u>form</u> to buy our house.
   a. paper   b. book   c. name

4. After I finished eating, my plate was <u>bare</u>.
   a. large animal   b. empty   c. plenty

5. I <u>like</u> wearing skirts because they are pretty when I twirl.
   a. spin   b. don't like   c. enjoy

6. The surface of the water was <u>calm</u> until it began to rain.
   a. stormy   b. still   c. wavy

7. Khalil liked the <u>glory</u> of winning the city's big race.
   a. honor   b. flag   c. medal

8. My friend and I are <u>opposites</u>, but we still have fun together.
   a. happy   b. exactly alike   c. not alike

Context Clues

Use context clues to figure out the meaning of each underlined word below. Circle the correct meaning. Use a dictionary to help as needed.

1. Shelby is on a quest to find her watch.
   a. wheel
   b. race
   c. search

2. Two world wars were fought during the twentieth century.
   a. season
   b. period of 100 years
   c. month

3. The first 13 US states formed a union so that they could be stronger.
   a. separation
   b. president
   c. single governing body

4. In the story, the fox chased the hare across the field.
   a. rabbit
   b. frog
   c. something on your head

5. In our society, everyone must follow certain laws.
   a. house
   b. community
   c. rules

6. Todd ate lunch in the pause between speakers.
   a. break
   b. animals' feet
   c. nap

7. Iesha exclaimed in a loud voice, "I got an A on the test!"
   a. sang
   b. read
   c. shouted

8. Seth glanced at my friend across the classroom.
   a. words
   b. looked
   c. spoke

9. The effect of staying up all night was that I fell asleep at breakfast.
   a. result
   b. cause
   c. change

Answer Key

Drawing Conclusions

Read the story. Then, answer the questions.

Dad's Trumpet

Owen's dad played the trumpet when he was in school. He led the marching band and had a solo in every concert. Owen wanted to play the trumpet too. One day at Grandma's house, he found a dusty case in the closet of his dad's old room. It was Dad's old trumpet! Grandma said that Owen could try it out, so Owen put the instrument to his lips. He blew as hard as he could, but there was no sound. Grandma showed him how to buzz his lips on the mouthpiece, and finally the trumpet made a noise. It sounded nothing like the players Owen had heard in the band. Owen felt sad. He guessed he did not have his dad's talent. He was about to put the trumpet away, when Grandma stopped him. She smiled and said, "You sound just like your dad did when he first started playing. Don't give up yet!"

1. What clues do you have that Owen's dad was a good trumpet player?

   He led the marching band and had a solo in every concert.

2. Why does Owen want to play the trumpet?

   To be like his dad.

3. How can you tell that Dad does not play the trumpet anymore?

   It was at Grandma's house in a dusty case.

4. Why does Owen have a hard time playing the trumpet?

   He does not know how to play yet.

5. Why does Grandma tell Owen not to give up yet?

   His dad had to practice to be a good player, and Owen

   will too.

6. What do you think Owen will do next?

   Answers will vary.

Drawing Conclusions

Read the story. Then, answer the questions.

The Long Hike

Jorge and his friends decided to go on a hike Saturday morning. They wanted to reach the top of a nearby hill so that they could see the whole town. His dad asked if he had remembered to pack water and a snack for the trail. Jorge was in a hurry, but he stopped to pick up a bottle of water and a packet of trail mix for his backpack. He thought they would be back before he got thirsty or hungry, but it took them more time to get to the top of the hill than he had expected. When they stopped to rest, he heard his stomach growl. The view was nice. Jorge and his friends sat down and ate the snack. When they finished, they jogged down the trail. When they got to the bottom of the hill, Jorge saw his mom's car pull up. She rolled down the window and said with a smile, "Ready for lunch?"

1. Why do Jorge and his friends want to hike up the hill?

   To see the whole town from the top.

2. How can you tell Jorge's parents want him to be careful on the trail?

   His dad asks if he has water and a snack.

3. What does Jorge take with him?

   His backpack and some water and trail mix.

4. How can you tell Jorge is glad he brought food and water?

   He hears his stomach growl and stops to have a snack.

5. Why does Jorge's mom come to meet him?

   Jorge's mom meets them because she thinks that they might

   be hungry and ready for lunch.

6. What do you think Jorge will do the next time he goes on a hike?

   Answers will vary.

Drawing Conclusions

Read the story. Then, answer the questions.

Soup Kitchen

Rashad's parents liked to help other people. His mom made recordings of books for the blind, and his dad built new houses for people who could not afford them. Rashad's mother said that they should have Thanksgiving dinner at the soup kitchen. Rashad's dad said that was an excellent idea. Rashad did not know what a soup kitchen was. He liked soup, so maybe it was a place to try lots of different kinds. But they usually ate turkey and stuffing at Thanksgiving. He did not think that soup would taste as good. On Thanksgiving Day, Rashad helped his dad carry boxes to the car. They held canned goods, fresh vegetables, and even a turkey! When they got to the soup kitchen, Rashad discovered that there was more than just soup. The soup kitchen was a place where people could come for dinner if they had no food of their own. Rashad's parents were helping serve dinner. Rashad helped too, and he thought it was the best Thanksgiving ever.

1. How do Rashad's parents help others?

   His mom reads books for the blind; his dad builds houses.

2. What does Rashad think a soup kitchen is?

   a place to try different kinds of soup

3. What does Rashad's family usually eat at Thanksgiving?

   They usually eat turkey and stuffing.

4. What clues tell you what a soup kitchen really is?

   Rashad's parents like to help people, and they carry boxes of

   food to the car.

5. How do Rashad's parents help at the soup kitchen?

   They bring boxes of food and serve dinner.

6. How can you tell Rashad likes helping people too?

   He thinks that it is the best Thanksgiving ever.

Drawing Conclusions

Read the story. Then, answer the questions.

Training Jake

Lucy had a playful dog named Jake. He liked to grab her toys and run away from her. When Jake was a puppy, it was easy to catch him. As Jake grew bigger, Lucy had to shout for him to come back. Neither of them was having much fun. Lucy's mom thought Jake should go to obedience training. A trainer could show Lucy how to make Jake obey her. Lucy found a class that met at the park on Saturday mornings. She walked Jake down to the park, but she felt like Jake was walking her! He was so strong, she could hardly hold him back. At the park, the other dogs were already sitting politely in a circle. The trainer smiled when Jake and Lucy ran up. She said, "Jake has a lot of energy! I can help both of you learn how to control it."

1. Why is Jake's behavior becoming a problem as he gets bigger?

   Lucy cannot catch him when he runs away with her toys.

2. What clues tell you that training will be good for both Jake and Lucy?

   Neither of them has fun when Lucy shouts at Jake.

3. When and where does the class meet?

   Saturday mornings at the park

4. Why does Lucy feel like Jake is walking her?

   He is so strong, she can hardly hold him back.

5. How can you tell the other dogs already know some commands?

   They are already sitting politely in a circle.

6. Will the trainer be able to help Jake? Why or why not?

   Answers will vary.

Answer Key

Name_____ 3.RL.1, 3.RL.3, 3.RL.10

Drawing Conclusions
Read the story. Then, answer the questions.

A Painting for Mom

Mario loved to paint. He was always asking Mom for money to spend on supplies like brushes and special paper. Sometimes, Mom said that Mario had an expensive talent. Mario was walking home one day when he saw a sign about a city art contest. The topic was "What My Mom Means to Me." The winner would receive a cash prize! Mario thought about all of the art supplies he could buy if he won. As soon as he got home, he got out his paints and brushes. He thought about everything Mom did for their family. She cooked healthy food for him and his sister. She drove them to swimming classes in the summer. She worked hard so that they could buy new shoes when they grew out of their old ones. Mario smiled and started to paint. Now, he had a new idea for what to do with the money if he won.

1. What is Mario doing?
   painting a picture for an art contest

2. Why does Mom say Mario's art talent is expensive?
   He always needs money for art supplies.

3. What will the winner of the art contest receive?
   a cash prize

4. What does Mario want to do with the prize money?
   buy art supplies

5. What does Mom do for Mario's family?
   Mom cooks healthy food, drives them to swimming classes, and buys them new shoes.

6. What might be Mario's new idea for the money at the end of the story?
   Answers will vary.

© Carson-Dellosa • CD-104621 — 9

Name_____ 3.RL.1, 3.RL.3, 3.RL.10

Drawing Conclusions
Read the story. Then, answer the questions.

Family Photos

Malia's father had accepted a new job across the country. He would be leaving soon. Malia and her mother would be staying in their old house until school was out. Malia would miss her friends when they moved, but she would miss her dad more. Her mother pretended to be cheerful, but Malia knew she would be lonely too. Sometimes, she caught her mom looking at old photos with a tear in her eye. She decided to make something that would remind both her mom and her dad that they had a strong family. One afternoon, Malia took the box of family photos up to her room. She cut out two large cardboard hearts. Then, she picked out pictures of herself, her mom, and her dad. She glued the pictures to the hearts. At the top of each heart she wrote "A Family Is Love." Now Dad would have pictures to remember them by, and Mom would not be so sad when she looked at the photos.

1. Why is Malia's father moving without them?
   Her father has a new job across the country.
   Malia will finish the school year at home.

2. Who will Malia miss the most?
   Malia will miss her dad the most.

3. Why does Mom pretend to be cheerful?
   She does not want Malia to be sad.

4. What clues do you have that Mom is not really cheerful?
   She cries when she looks at old photos.

5. Why does Malia cut out two cardboard hearts?
   Malia cuts out the hearts so she can give one to her mom and one to her dad.

6. Why will Mom be less sad when she looks at photos now?
   The photos will remind her that their family is strong.

10 — © Carson-Dellosa • CD-104621

Name_____ 3.RL.1, 3.RL.3, 3.RL.10

Drawing Conclusions
Read the story. Then, answer the questions.

Alicia's Song

Alicia had been practicing for weeks. She sang in the shower, in her bedroom, and on the way to school. Her teacher said that she was ready to sing in a concert, but Alicia was not sure. Mom had taken her to buy a new dress. She helped Alicia curl her hair. Alicia thought she would feel calm when she walked out onto the stage, but her palms were sweaty and her shoes felt too tight. She hoped she would not forget the words. Alicia heard the applause for the performer before her. Her friend Chelsea walked off the stage and whispered, "You're on!" Chelsea patted Alicia's shoulder and said, "Good luck!" Alicia took a deep breath and walked out into the spotlight. Finally, it was time for her solo. She saw Mom and her teacher smiling at her from the front row and knew she would do well.

1. What is Alicia doing?
   performing a song in public

2. How long has Alicia been practicing?
   for weeks

3. What clues tell you how Alicia feels?
   She is nervous. Her palms are sweaty, and her shoes feel tight. She hopes she will not forget the words.

4. How did Mom help Alicia prepare?
   She bought her a new dress and curled her hair.

5. What does Chelsea do to help Alicia?
   She pats her shoulder and wishes her good luck.

6. How does Alicia feel at the end of the story? How do you know?
   Alicia feels calm. She sees Mom and her teacher smiling at her from the front row and knows she will do well.

© Carson-Dellosa • CD-104621 — 11

Name_____ 3.RL.1, 3.RL.3, 3.RL.10

Drawing Conclusions
Read the story. Then, answer the questions.

Dad's Day

Dad's birthday was in June, near Father's Day. Sometimes, they were even on the same day. Isabelle and Hector thought it was unfair when their dad only had one special day in June. Their friends' dads had a Father's Day party in June and a birthday party in a different month. Isabelle thought of a way to fix this problem. They would surprise Dad in autumn with Dad's Day. Hector talked to their mom about cooking a special breakfast. She showed him how to cook eggs and bacon. Isabelle made a special card for Dad. They were careful to keep their plans secret. One day in October, Isabelle and Hector woke up early and crept downstairs. They cooked Dad's breakfast and took it upstairs with their card. Dad loved his surprise. He said that he hoped they could have Dad's Day every weekend!

1. Why do Isabelle and Hector want to have a Dad's Day?
   Their dad's birthday is close to Father's Day, so he only has one special day in June.

2. Why are Dad's birthday and Father's Day on the same day only sometimes?
   Father's Day is not on the same day every year.

3. What does Hector do to prepare?
   learns how to cook eggs and bacon

4. What does Isabelle do to prepare?
   makes a special card for Dad

5. Why do Isabelle and Hector keep their plans secret?
   They keep their plans secret because they want Dad to be surprised.

6. Why does Dad want to have Dad's Day every weekend?
   He enjoyed having breakfast in bed.

12 — © Carson-Dellosa • CD-104621

Answer Key

Name_____   (3.RL.1, 3.RL.3, 3.RL.10)

Drawing Conclusions

Read the story. Then, answer the questions.

Lamar's Tomato Garden

One day, Lamar's class took a field trip to a greenhouse. The students were amazed at how many different plants were growing in the building. They saw plump tomatoes and lovely pink orchids. The gardener explained that she kept the greenhouse warm and misty so that the plants could grow better. She said that it was easier to grow plants inside the greenhouse, where they were not in danger from bad weather or pests. When Lamar got home from school, he told his mother all about the greenhouse. He asked if they could build one in their backyard. Wouldn't it be great to have fresh tomatoes year-round? Mom said, "A greenhouse sounds like fun, but it can be a lot of work. Why don't you grow some tomatoes in a pot first to see if you have a green thumb." Lamar decided to try. He would grow so many tomatoes that they would need a greenhouse to hold them all!

1. What kinds of plants did Lamar's class see?

Lamar's class saw tomatoes and orchids.

2. Why are greenhouses good places to grow plants?

Greenhouses are warm and misty; and protect plants from

bad weather and pests.

3. What does Lamar want to do?

Lamar wants to build a greenhouse in his backyard.

4. What does Mom suggest?

Lamar should try growing tomatoes in a pot first.

5. What does it mean to have a green thumb?

Having a green thumb means you grow things well.

6. What does Lamar decide to do at the end of the story?

Lamar is going to try to grow so many tomatoes that they

will have to build a greenhouse.

© Carson-Dellosa • CD-104621   13

Name_____   (3.RL.1, 3.RL.10)

Predicting

Read each story. Then, answer the questions.

Sandra's mother offered to help her get ready for the new school year. Sandra had grown a full inch taller over the summer. Her shoes were too tight, and her pants were almost above her ankles.

1. What do you think Sandra and her mother will do?

shop for new school clothes

2. Which clues helped you decide?

Sandra had grown taller over the summer, her shoes were

too tight, and her pants were too short.

When Ahmad got home from school, he could not find his cat. Ahmad called out his cat's name, but his cat did not come. Ahmad looked in his closet. He looked under his bed. Just then, Ahmad heard his mom drive up. She was home from work. Ahmad was glad his mom was home.

3. What do you think Ahmad will do?

ask his mom to help look for his cat

4. Which clues helped you decide?

He looked in many places but couldn't find his cat and his

mom was home now.

Mandy tried out for the school track team. She wore her favorite shoes and came in first in her race. The gym teacher posted the results the day after the tryouts. Mandy raced to the gym to see the list of who had made the team.

5. What do you think will happen next?

Mandy will make the track team.

6. Which clues helped you decide?

Mandy won her race.

14   © Carson-Dellosa • CD-104621

Name_____   (3.RL.1, 3.RL.10)

Predicting

Read the story. Then, answer the questions.

Miguel needed to write a book report. He finished reading the book and began to plan his paper. The report was worth two test grades, so it was important for him to do well. Miguel's mom said that he had a phone call. It was his friend Tony, who wanted to play video games.

1. What do you think will happen next?

Miguel will finish his report instead of going to Tony's house.

2. Which clues helped you decide?

He was planning his report, and it is worth two test grades,

so he wants to do well.

Yuri laid his head on his desk. His face felt hot, and the desk was nice and cool. Yuri's class was supposed to have an ice cream party that afternoon. Yuri thought the ice cream would feel good to his sore throat. Just then, his teacher said that she thought Yuri should go to the nurse's office.

3. What do you think will happen next?

The nurse will send him home and he will miss the party.

4. Which clues helped you decide?

His face is hot and his throat is sore, so he should go home.

Tia and her brother Trey decided to go hiking. They wore sturdy shoes and light clothing. They put on hats and plenty of sunscreen. They had just reached the top of a tall, rocky hill when they heard a clap of thunder. The sky grew dark. Trey spotted a cave in the side of the hill.

5. What do you think will happen next?

They will stay in the cave until the storm passes.

6. Which clues helped you decide?

The sky is dark and they heard thunder, so it is going to storm.

Trey saw a cave in the side of the hill that they can shelter in.

© Carson-Dellosa • CD-104621   15

Name_____   (3.RL.1, 3.RL.10)

Predicting

Read each story. Then, answer the questions.

Amy's teacher told the class to close their math books. They were having a pop test! Amy was surprised. She was happy that she had studied the chapter the night before. She had not understood the problems in class, so she had asked her mother for extra help. Amy took out a sheet of paper and wrote her name at the top.

1. What do you think will happen next?

Amy will do well on the test.

2. Which clues helped you decide?

She had studied the chapter the night before.

Seth came home from school and prepared himself a sandwich. He put some slices of meat and cheese on it with extra mustard. Seth put his sandwich on a plate and took it to the living room. He thought he would watch his favorite TV show while he ate. His dog came in to see what Seth was doing. Seth set his sandwich on the table and went back into the kitchen for a glass of milk.

3. What do you think will happen next?

Seth's dog will steal his sandwich.

4. Which clues helped you decide?

Seth has left his sandwich behind to get a glass of milk, and

his dog is alone in the room with his sandwich.

Sarah went to her uncle's farm to visit her cousin Kami. Sarah and Kami were the same age and wore the same size. Sometimes, people thought they were twins! Kami wanted to go fishing, so she told Sarah to put on old jeans. Then, Sarah realized she had forgotten her suitcase.

5. What do you think will happen next?

Kami will lend Sarah some old clothes.

6. Which clues helped you decide?

The cousins wore the same size so they can share clothes.

16   © Carson-Dellosa • CD-104621

© Carson-Dellosa • CD-104621

Answer Key

Name _____ 3.RL.1, 3.RL.10

Predicting

Read the story. Then, answer the questions.

Raul wanted to earn money this summer. He was tired of asking for change to buy comic books and candy. His best friend, Shane, lived next door. Shane and his family were going to be gone all summer. Shane's family could not travel on the plane with their two dogs.

1. What do you think Raul will do?

He will offer to take care of Shane's dogs for the summer.

2. Which clues helped you decide?

He wants to earn money over the summer. Shane's family

could not take the dogs on vacation with them.

Jan's family was moving to a new town with their orange and white cat. Sadly, the cat ran away when they were moving boxes from the truck to the house. Two weeks later, the cat still had not returned. Jan was very sad. She missed her cat. Her new friend Arifa, who lived next door, called Jan one morning to say that she had just seen an orange and white cat in her yard.

3. What do you think will happen next?

Jan will find her cat.

4. Which clues helped you decide?

Arifa saw the same color cat in her yard.

Felicia wanted to surprise her mom with a cake. With Grandma's help, she mixed the ingredients and put the batter in a pan. She turned on the oven and put the pan inside. She set a timer and waited for the cake to bake. Felicia's mom came home early and called, "What is that wonderful smell?"

5. What do you think will happen next?

Felicia will surprise her mom with the cake.

6. Which clues helped you decide?

Felicia's mom came home early. The cake was a surprise.

© Carson-Dellosa • CD-104621   17

Name _____ 3.RL.1, 3.RL.10

Predicting

Read the story. Then, answer the questions.

Jason stood at the top of the ladder to the diving board. His knees felt wobbly, and his hands were sweaty. He walked out onto the board. It was a long way down. Just then, he heard his sister shout, "Come on, Jason! You can do it!" He took a deep breath.

1. What do you think Jason will do?

He will dive off the diving board.

2. Which clues helped you decide?

His sister shouted encouragement so that made him feel

good. He took a deep breath, so he is preparing to dive off.

Quan's stepdad was working late every night. He had not gotten home before dark for the past month. Quan noticed that the yard was covered in dead leaves. He knew his mom did not like it. She had hurt her leg and could not stand up for very long. Quan wanted to help.

3. What do you think Quan will do?

Quan will rake the yard and bag up the leaves.

4. Which clues helped you decide?

Quan wants to help. His stepdad is working late and his

mom hurt her leg, so they can't rake the leaves.

Jayla took piano lessons. She liked to play for her mom every night after dinner. Sometimes, her friends came over to sing while she played. Jayla's piano teacher was having a party for all of her students the next week. She wanted all of her students to play for each other, and one would win a prize.

5. What do you think will happen next?

Jayla will play well and win a prize.

6. Which clues helped you decide?

Jayla plays piano often, so she is probably very good.

18   © Carson-Dellosa • CD-104621

Name _____ 3.RL.1, 3.RL.10

Predicting

Read the story. Then, answer the questions in complete sentences.

Tara found a pair of sunglasses on the bus. They were bright pink with red lightning bolts on the earpieces. Tara felt like a rock star wearing them. After lunch, Tara put on the sunglasses to go out for recess. An older girl ran up to her and said, "Excuse me, but I think that those are mine." Tara's heart sank.

1. What do you think Tara will do?

Tara will give them back.

2. Which clues helped you decide?

Tara's heart sank, so she knows she should give them back.

Ray wanted to play football more than anything else in the world. There was a new team starting in his neighborhood, and he wanted to try out. His family was concerned that if Ray joined the team, he would not have time to do his homework. His family wanted Ray to have fun, but they also wanted him to do well in school. Ray was sure that he would have time to do his homework and play on the team.

3. What do you think will happen next?

Ray's family will let him play football if he keeps his grades up.

4. Which clues helped you decide?

His family wants him to have fun and do well in school.

Ivy's grandmother was celebrating her 70th birthday soon. Ivy wanted to get her grandmother a special gift, but she had spent her money on new books instead. Ivy loved reading books about Mexico. Her grandmother had come from Mexico, and she used to read to Ivy when she was little. Lately, her grandmother's eyesight had been failing, and she could no longer see the words on the page.

5. What do you think Ivy will do?

Ivy will read books about Mexico to her grandmother as a gift.

6. Which clues helped you decide?

Ivy's grandmother cannot see so Ivy can read for her. They

both like to read about Mexico so it will be fun for Ivy, too.

© Carson-Dellosa • CD-104621   19

Name _____ 3.RI.3, 3.RI.8, 3.RI.10

Cause and Effect

Read the story. Then, answer the questions.

Saguaro Cactus

In the Arizona desert, a cactus grows that will live 100 years or more. The saguaro cactus grows very slowly in the hot, dry desert, and it becomes home to many animals as it grows.

The cactus starts as a seed dropped from the fruit of a mature saguaro cactus. The seed sprouts after a rare rain gives it moisture. It swells up, splits its shell, and sends a root down into the soil. Then, the seed sends up a stem.

It does not rain often in the desert, so the stem grows slowly. After one year, it has grown less than a centimeter. After 10 years, it may be only 15 centimeters (6 inches) tall. When it is 50 years old, the original stem is about 4 1/2 meters (15 feet) high. After 50 years, the saguaro cactus finally grows its first branches.

Many animals make their homes in the saguaro cactus. Animals like its moist skin. Animals like woodpeckers, mice, hawks, and owls can live in the cactus.

Beautiful flowers grow on the mature saguaro cactus. The flowers provide juicy nectar for birds, insects, and bats. After the flowers dry up, green fruits cover the cactus. Many animals come to eat the fruit. They spread the seeds from the fruit onto the ground where the seeds wait for rain. Eventually these seeds will sprout and grow new saguaro cactuses. The cycle goes on and on for hundreds of years.

1. What causes a saguaro cactus seed to sprout?

moisture from a rare rain

2. What causes the cactus stem to grow so slowly?

It does not rain often in the desert.

3. What happens because the cactus has moist skin?

Many animals make their homes in the cactus.

4. What must happen before the seeds can sprout and grow new cactuses?

animals spread the seeds and it rains

5. Why do you think the cactus grows flowers and fruit?

Answers will vary but may include to attract animals that

spread its seeds.

20   © Carson-Dellosa • CD-104621

© Carson-Dellosa • CD-104621

107

Answer Key

Name _____   3.RI.3, 3.RI.8, 3.RI.10

Cause and Effect

Read the story. Then, answer the questions.

Tipi

For centuries, people have lived on the Great Plains. This is flat grassland with few trees. Many animals used to roam here. Humans would follow them to hunt. People needed homes they could quickly tear down and set up. Tribes such as the Arapaho, Pawnee, Blackfoot, Sioux, and Cheyenne used tipis. Tipis were made of wood poles and buffalo hides. When buffalo became scarce, Plains people used canvas cloth instead.

The first step in making a tipi was to prepare the poles. They had to be long and straight. The best trees to use were willow, lodgepole pine, and cedar. When people traveled, the poles dragged on the ground. They wore out and had to be replaced.

The women prepared the buffalo hides. First, they scraped each hide. Then they soaked the hides with water to soften them. Next, they sewed the hides together in the shape of a half circle. They cut a hole for the door and created smoke flaps. Finally, they fitted the cover over the frame and lit a fire inside. The smoke preserved the skin.

In the late 1800s, roads and cities were built. Many of the Plains people were forced to live on reservations. They no longer lived in tipis. Still, the tipi remains an important part of Native American culture today.

1. What caused the Plains people to move around so much?
They followed the buffalo.

2. How did their lifestyle of moving affect their style of home?
They needed portable homes.

3. What caused them to use canvas instead of buffalo hides for tipi covers?
The buffalo were hunted until they became scarce.

4. What was the effect on the poles when they were dragged on the ground?
They wore out and had to be replaced.

5. What was the effect of water on the buffalo hides?
It softened the hides.

6. On a seperate sheet of paper, explain why you think it is important to preserve the culture of the Plains people. **Answers will vary.**

© Carson-Dellosa • CD-104621   21

Name _____   3.RI.3, 3.RI.8, 3.RI.10

Cause and Effect

Read the story. Then, answer the questions in complete sentences.

Yellowstone Fires

In 1988, a huge fire burned nearly half of Yellowstone National Park. This was a healthy part of the forest's natural life cycle. The forests had been growing for centuries. Many trees had died. Their trunks fell on the ground and remained there. Eventually the ground was covered with dead trees. This blocked the sun from new growth on the forest floor. It also made it difficult for animals to travel. There were fewer meadows for new plants, and animals had less grazing area.

Lightning started several fires that summer. The dead tree trunks on the forest floor ignited like firewood. Firefighters were able to protect some areas from burning but the fires did not stop until snow fell.

After the fires were out, the forests began to grow again. Some roots and seeds had remained safe underground. Others, like lodgepole pine seeds, had been locked in cones that the heat had released. Beautiful new plants grew. This provided perfect food for the animals. Many of the surviving animals live in the meadows that now cover much of the park. More than half of the park was untouched, so there are still forests.

Yellowstone continues to recover. As the park evolves, new animals and plants find their homes there. In about 300 years, the park will be ready for a new fire to give it a fresh start once again.

1. What is an effect of a fire on trees and plants in a forest?
Answers will vary.

2. What is an effect on the forest if there are no fires for years?
Answers will vary.

3. What caused the fires to spread so quickly?
Everything was dry, so the dead trees on the ground ignited.

4. What will be the effect of 300 more years of growth?
After 300 years of growth, another fire will be needed to control the growth.

5. Was the effect of the Yellowstone fires positive or negative? Explain your answer.
The effect of the fires was positive. Explanations will vary.

22   © Carson-Dellosa • CD-104621

Name _____   3.RI.1, 3.RI.2, 3.RI.10

Main Idea

Read the story. Then, answer the questions.

Martin Luther King, Jr.

Martin Luther King, Jr., was an important leader in the U.S. civil rights movement. This movement forced leaders to change unfair laws so that all people would be treated fairly, regardless of their skin color. King was born in 1929 in Atlanta, Georgia. In 1954, King became the leader of a church in Montgomery, Alabama. During this time, African Americans were told that they had to give up their bus seats if a white person wanted to sit down. King and others refused to ride the buses at all until they were given equal treatment. In 1963, he led a march in Washington, D.C., to ask the government to change the laws so that everyone was treated fairly. King received the Nobel Peace Prize in 1964 for his work. He traveled to Memphis, Tennessee, in 1968 to give a speech in support of equal wages. He was shot on April 4. Although King died, his ideas on freedom and equality live on today.

1. What is the main idea of this story?
(a.) Martin Luther King, Jr., was a great civil rights leader.
b. Martin Luther King, Jr., led a march in 1963.
c. Martin Luther King, Jr., was born in 1929.

2. Why did King lead a march in Washington, D.C.?
to ask the government to change the laws so everyone was treated fairly

3. Circle the correct word in parentheses to complete each sentence.
a. King led a march to Washington, D.C. ((after) before) he became the leader of a church in Montgomery, Alabama.
b. King received the Nobel Peace Prize (after, (before)) he traveled to Memphis, Tennessee to give an important speech.
c. King was shot (after, (before)) he gave his speech in support of equal wages.

4. Why do you think King received the Nobel Peace Prize in 1964? On a separate sheet of paper, write a paragraph explaining your opinion.
Check students' writing.

© Carson-Dellosa • CD-104621   23

Name _____   3.RI.1, 3.RI.2, 3.RI.10

Main Idea

Read the story. Then, answer the questions.

James Naismith

Have you ever played basketball with your friends? You dribble the ball, run down the court, and shoot it through a hoop. The modern game of basketball was invented by James Naismith in 1891. Naismith was a Canadian gym teacher. He wanted a game that would not take up too much room. He wanted to be able to play it indoors. Naismith nailed peach baskets at both ends of the gym. Then, he sorted his players into two teams of nine each. The players passed a ball to each other. Then, they threw it into the basket when they reached the end of the court. Eventually, players started to bounce the ball instead of just tossing it to each other. This bouncing motion became known as dribbling. Basketball soon caught on among both men's and women's teams. It became an official Olympic sport in 1936, and Naismith was invited to watch. Naismith died in 1939, but his sport lives on. Over 300 million people around the world play basketball today.

1. What is the main idea of this story?
a. James Naismith's sport lives on today.
b. James Naismith was a gym teacher.
(c.) James Naismith invented the sport of basketball.

2. What did the first basketball hoops look like?
peach baskets

3. What kind of game did Naismith want to invent?
an indoor game that didn't take much room to play

4. Circle the correct word in parentheses to complete each sentence.
a. Basketball was invented (after, (before)) 1908.
b. Basketball became an Olympic Sport (after, (before)) Naismith died.
c. In the original basketball game, players passed the ball to each other directly (after, (before)) they threw the ball into the basket.

5. Do you think that basketball is still popular today? On a separate sheet of paper, write a paragraph explaining your opinion.
Check students' writing.

24   © Carson-Dellosa • CD-104621

Answer Key

Main Idea
Read the story. Then, answer the questions.

Lucy Maud Montgomery

Lucy Maud Montgomery is a famous Canadian author. Her most loved character is Anne Shirley in the widely read series Anne of Green Gables. Montgomery was born in 1874 on Prince Edward Island. She lived with her grandparents. Montgomery went to class in a one-room schoolhouse. At age 17, her first poem was published. Montgomery taught at three island schools. She took courses at a university in nearby Nova Scotia. Montgomery wrote Anne of Green Gables in 1905. It was not published until 1908. The book became a bestseller. Montgomery wrote several other books based on the main character. Two films and at least seven TV shows have been made from the Anne books. Although Montgomery moved away in 1911, all but one of her books is set in Prince Edward Island. Many people today still visit the island to see where "Anne Shirley" grew up.

1. What is the main idea of this story?
   a. Lucy Maud Montgomery grew up on Prince Edward Island.
   b. Lucy Maud Montgomery is famous for writing Anne of Green Gables.
   c. Lucy Maud Montgomery was a schoolteacher.

2. Who is Anne Shirley?

   the main character in Montgomery's Anne of Green Gables

   series

3. Give at least two reasons the author gives that Anne of Green Gables was a popular book.
   Answers will vary.

4. Circle the correct word in parentheses to complete each sentence.
   a. Anne of Green Gables was published (after, before) Montgomery moved away from Prince Edward Island.
   b. Montgomery lived with her grandparents (before, while) attending university in Nova Scotia.
   c. Montgomery's first poem was published (after, before) 1905.

5. Why do you think many people visit Prince Edward Island today? On a separate sheet of paper, write a paragraph explaining your opinion.

   Check students' writing.

Main Idea
Read the story. Then, answer the questions.

Amelia Earhart

Amelia Earhart is a famous airplane pilot. She was the first woman to fly across the Atlantic Ocean. Earhart was born in 1897. She saw her first plane at the Iowa state fair at age 10. Earhart studied to be a nurse and then a social worker. But she was always interested in flight. She started taking flying lessons in 1921. The first plane Earhart bought was bright yellow. She called it Canary. In 1928, Earhart flew from Canada to Wales. She crossed the Atlantic Ocean in only 21 hours. When she returned to the United States, a parade was held in her honor. Earhart crossed the Atlantic again in 1932. This time she flew by herself. The U.S. Congress gave her a special medal for this accomplishment. The medal is called the Distinguished Flying Cross. Earhart continued to set new records. In 1937 she decided to fly around the world. Her plane was lost over the Pacific Ocean. Amelia Earhart was never heard from again.

1. What is the main idea of this story?
   a. Amelia Earhart flew around the world.
   b. Amelia Earhart was a brave woman who flew airplanes.
   c. Amelia Earhart had a yellow plane called Canary.

2. Why do you think Earhart called her first plane Canary?
   it was bright yellow like a canary bird

3. You can tell a lot about people by what they do. Circle the adjective(s) that you think describe Amelia Earhart. Use a dictionary if necessary.
   (adventurous)   timid   (popular)   (determined)

4. What do you think happened to Earhart in 1937? Use an encyclopedia, the Internet, and maps to learn about that area in the Pacific Ocean. On a separate sheet of paper, write a paragraph explaining your opinion.

   Check students' writing.

Main Idea
Read the story. Then, answer the questions.

Roberto Clemente

Roberto Clemente was born in Puerto Rico in 1934. As a child, he played baseball in his neighborhood. He also played for his high school team. At 16, he joined a junior national league. He played baseball briefly in Canada before signing to play for the Pittsburgh Pirates in 1954. Clemente served in the U.S. Marine Reserves for several years. This helped him grow physically stronger. He later helped the Pirates win two World Series. During the off-season, Clemente often went back to Puerto Rico to help. He liked visiting children in hospitals. He gave them hope that they could get well. In 1972, an earthquake hit the country of Nicaragua. Clemente helped out there, too. He was on his way to deliver supplies to Nicaragua when he died in a plane crash. He was 38 years old. Clemente was elected to the Baseball Hall of Fame in 1973. He was the first Hispanic player to receive the honor.

1. What is the main idea of this story?
   a. Roberto Clemente was a great baseball player who also helped people.
   b. Roberto Clemente died in a plane crash.
   c. Roberto Clemente elected to the Baseball Hall of Fame.

2. You can tell a lot about people by what they do. Circle the adjective(s) that you think describe Roberto Clemente. Use a dictionary if necessary.
   (athletic)   (caring)   (persistent)   selfish

3. Circle the correct word in parentheses to complete each sentence.
   a. Clemente served in the U.S. Marine Reserves (after, before) he played baseball in Canada.
   b. Clemente's team won the World Series (before, after) he was voted into the Baseball Hall of Fame.
   c. The plane crash occurred (after, before) the Venezuelan earthquake.

4. What visual aid (e.g., maps, photographs) would help you better understand this story? Why?
   Answers will vary.

5. Clemente died while helping with relief efforts in the Central American country of Nicaragua. If you were famous, do you think you would want to help in that way? Why or why not? On a separate sheet of paper, write a paragraph explaining your opinion.

   Check students' writing.

Main Idea
Read the story. Then, answer the questions.

Titanic

In the spring of 1912, the Titanic set off from England. This was its first journey. The Titanic was a luxury ship headed for New York City. But its journey across the icy Atlantic Ocean was cut short. Around midnight on April 14, the ship hit an iceberg. In less than three hours the ship had sunk. Over 700 people survived. However, more than 1,500 lives were lost. Because of the way the Titanic was built, everyone thought it was impossible for the ship to sink. This certainty led to several of the causes of the disaster. We now know that the captain had ignored warnings of ice. He pushed the Titanic too fast through dangerous waters. We also know that there were not enough lifeboats on board. Because of the Titanic disaster, new rules were set. Now people know that every ship can sink, so ships must carry enough lifeboats for everyone on board.

1. What is the main idea of this story?
   a. The Titanic was unsinkable.
   b. The sinking of the Titanic was a huge disaster.
   c. A ship called the Titanic left England in 1912.

2. What does the phrase cut short in this story mean?
   stopped before it was supposed to

3. What does the story say contributed to, or caused, the disaster?
   Answers will vary.

4. Circle the correct word in parentheses to complete each sentence.
   a. The Titanic sank (after, before) it left England.
   b. The captain received warnings of ice (after, before) the Titanic hit an iceberg.
   c. Over 700 people aboard the Titanic survived (after, before) their ship sank.

5. What visual aid (e.g., maps, photographs) would help you better understand this story? Why?
   Answers will vary.

6. What do you think might have happened if the Titanic had enough lifeboats for everyone? On a separate sheet of paper, write a paragraph explaining your opinion.
   Check students' writing.

Answer Key

Main Idea
Read the story. Then, answer the questions.

Thomas Jefferson

Thomas Jefferson was an important figure in early U.S. history. He was born in 1743 in the colony of Virginia. He became a lawyer. Jefferson grew active in the government of the new country that would become the United States. In 1776, he helped write the U.S. Declaration of Independence. This document said that the American colonies were no longer tied to Great Britain. Jefferson served as governor of Virginia. Then, he went to France to help strengthen ties between the two countries. Jefferson became the third president of the United States. He served two terms from 1801 to 1809. During his presidency, Jefferson authorized the Louisiana Purchase. This agreement expanded U.S. territory to include over 800,000 square miles (207,200,000 square kilometers) from Canada to the Gulf Coast. Jefferson died in 1826. Americans are reminded of him every time they spend a nickel. Jefferson's face is on one side. His home, Monticello, is on the other.

1. What is the main idea of this story?
   (a.) Thomas Jefferson was an important person in U.S. history.
   b. Thomas Jefferson's face is on the nickel.
   c. Thomas Jefferson was a lawyer.

2. You can tell a lot about people by what they say and do. Which sentence may have been said by Thomas Jefferson?
   a. "I love living in a British colony."
   b. "I don't think we should make this country any bigger."
   (c.) "I think friends and allies are important for a country."
   d. "I wrote the Declaration of Independence in about 10 minutes."

3. Which of the following sentences are true?
   (a.) Jefferson became president after 1800.
   (b.) The Declaration of Independence was written before the Louisiana Purchase occurred.
   (c.) Jefferson became governor of Virginia after he became a lawyer.
   d. Jefferson went to France before 1743.

4. Use resource books or the Internet to learn about the Louisiana Purchase. How did the Louisiana Purchase change the United States? Use a computer to type your research paper.
   Check students' writing.

Main Idea
Read the story. Then, answer the questions.

Babe Didrikson Zaharias

Babe Didrikson Zaharias was an outstanding sportswoman. She played golf, basketball, and baseball and also ran track. Zaharias grew up playing sports with her six brothers and sisters in Port Arthur, Texas. She played basketball with a company team when she worked as a secretary. She joined the U.S. Olympic team and won medals in three track-and-field events at the 1932 Olympics in Los Angeles. Zaharias began playing golf in 1935, and in 1938 she became the first woman to play in a PGA (Professional Golf Association) game. She became famous for her playing, and in 1950 she helped form the LPGA (Ladies Professional Golf Association). This group continues to hold golf matches for female golfers today. Zaharias died in 1956, but she was named to the U.S. Olympic Hall of Fame in 1983. People can learn more about Zaharias's life by visiting a museum in her honor in Beaumont, Texas.

1. What is the main idea of this story?
   a. Babe Didrikson Zaharias grew up in Texas.
   (b.) Babe Didrikson Zaharias was good at many sports.
   c. Babe Didrikson Zaharias died in 1956.

2. What happened to Zaharias at the 1932 Olympics?
   She won three medals in track and field.

3. In the sentence "This group continues to hold golf matches for female golfers today," what does the word *hold* mean?
   a. grab with their hands   (b.) arrange
   c. rest   d. stop

4. You can tell a lot about people by what they say and do. Which sentence may have been said by Babe Didrikson Zaharias?
   a. "I don't feel like exercising today."
   (b.) "It doesn't matter if you're a girl or a boy."
   c. "I would prefer to play a board game."
   d. "I'd much rather tie than win."

5. Use resource books or the Internet to learn about the LPGA. What does the LPGA do today? Use a computer to type your research paper. **Check students' writing.**

Main Idea
Read the story. Then, answer the questions.

Louisa May Alcott

For nearly 150 years, children have grown up reading about the March sisters. Meg, Jo, Beth, and Amy March are characters in the famous book *Little Women*. *Little Women* was written by Louisa May Alcott. Alcott grew up with three sisters in Massachusetts. In the book, the March sisters like to put on plays for their friends. Alcott and her sisters liked to do the same! Alcott's family was very poor. She helped them by working at many jobs. She was a maid, a teacher, a nurse, and a writer. Her books about the March family start with *Little Women*. These books were widely read during Alcott's lifetime. The main character, Jo, is based on Alcott herself. Jo works as a writer until she marries and has a family. Alcott continued to write until her death in 1888. She also spoke out for her beliefs. She supported women's rights. She was against slavery. Today, people can visit Orchard House, the home where Alcott grew up. It is also the place where *Little Women* is set.

1. What is the main idea of this story?
   a. Louisa May Alcott was very poor as a child.
   b. Louisa May Alcott had three sisters.
   (c.) Louisa May Alcott based her books on her own life.

2. What was Alcott known for besides writing?
   speaking out for women's rights and against slavery

3. In the sentence "These books were widely read during Alcott's lifetime," what does the phrase *widely read* mean?
   a. read by few people   b. taking up a lot of space
   c. not thin   (d.) read by many people

4. You can tell a lot about people by what they say and do. Which sentence may have been said by Louisa May Alcott?
   a. "I've run out of ideas on how to help my family."   b. "I'll buy the best that you have!"
   (c.) "All people are created equal."   d. "Why do I have to help?"

5. Use resource books or the Internet to learn about Louisa May Alcott and her family, and the March sisters from Little Women. Compare the Alcott family with the fictional March family. Use a computer to type your research paper.
   Check students' writing.

Main Idea
Read the story. Then, answer the questions.

Wayne Gretzky

Wayne Gretzky is called "The Great One" by fans of Canadian hockey. He scored over 1,000 goals during his career. Gretzky was born in Brantford, Ontario. He learned to ice-skate on his family's farm when he was three. Gretzky's father taught him and his three brothers to play hockey. They played on a frozen pond in the backyard. When Gretzky was six, he joined a league of 10-year-olds and began playing on a team. In the summer, he played baseball and lacrosse. His first professional hockey team was the Indianapolis Racers. He played for them when he was only 17. Then, he played for the Edmonton Oilers in Canada for nine years. During this time, they won hockey's Stanley Cup four times. He also played for several U.S. teams. Gretzky retired from the sport in 1999. He was voted into the Hockey Hall of Fame. Both his hometown of Brantford and his adopted city of Edmonton named streets after Gretzky to honor him.

1. What is the main idea of this story?
   (a.) Wayne Gretzky was a great hockey player.
   b. Wayne Gretzky had three brothers.
   c. Wayne Gretzky played hockey in the United States and Canada.

2. Where did Gretzky first play hockey?
   on a frozen pond in his backyard

3. What does the story say caused, the Edmonton Oilers to win the Stanley Cup so many times?
   Answers will vary.

4. Fans call Wayne Gretzky "The Great One" or "The Great Gretzky." Great Gretzky is an alliteration – the same sounds are repeated in nearby words. If Gretzky's name had been "Smith," people might have called him "Super Smith." On a separate sheet of paper, write down the names of three people that you admire. For each person, create at least two alliterations that show your admiration. Use any or all parts of their names. Write a sentence explaining each alliteration you chose.
   Check students' writing.

Answer Key

Name _____ 3.RI.1, 3.RI.2, 3.RI.10

Main Idea
Read the story. Then, answer the questions.

Lady Bird Johnson

Lady Bird Johnson was born as Claudia Taylor in 1912. A nurse said that Claudia was as pretty as a ladybird beetle. Ladybird is another name for a ladybug. So Lady Bird became her nickname. Lady Bird married Lyndon Baines Johnson in 1934. Together, they had two daughters. In 1963, President John F. Kennedy was killed. Lyndon Johnson became president of the United States. Lady Bird became First Lady. Most women who serve as First Lady choose a special project to work on. Lady Bird chose highway beautification. She wanted to make the highways of the United States more beautiful. She helped get millions of flowers planted. We can still see these flowers today. Lady Bird believed that "where flowers bloom, so does hope." She continued to help make her home state of Texas more beautiful after her husband left office. The Lady Bird Johnson Wildflower Center in Austin, Texas, was opened to help visitors learn about native plants.

1. What is the main idea of this story?
   a. Lady Bird Johnson was born in 1912.
   b. Lady Bird Johnson was married to a president.
   c. **Lady Bird Johnson helped make America's highways beautiful.**

2. How did Lady Bird get her nickname?
   A nurse said she was as pretty as a ladybird beetle.

3. How did Lady Bird become the First Lady?
   Her husband became president after President John F.
   Kennedy died.

4. Lady Bird believed that "where flowers bloom, so does hope." Did Lady Bird really believe that hope grew from a seed in the ground? Explain your answer.
   Answers will vary.

5. Use an encyclopedia or the Internet to learn about The Lady Bird Johnson Wildflower Center. What does this center do? On a separate sheet of paper, write a paragraph to tell about the Wildflower Center.
   Check students' writing.

© Carson-Dellosa • CD-104621   33

Name _____ 3.RI.1, 3.RI.2, 3.RI.10

Main Idea
Read the story. Then, answer the questions.

Edward R. Murrow

Edward R. Murrow was an American journalist. He was born in 1908 in North Carolina. After college, Murrow began working for a radio station. He became famous during the Second World War. In September 1939, London, England was bombed. This was known as the Blitz. Murrow was there! People all over America listened to his live broadcasts. Americans used to learn about the war only through newsreels in movie theaters or newspaper articles. Now, they could listen to Murrow on their radios at home. Murrow was very brave to risk his life so that Americans could learn about the war in London. When the war ended, Murrow continued to work as a radio reporter. Then he moved to television. On TV, he became known for interviewing. He would interview, or ask questions of, famous people. Other newscasters followed in Murrow's footsteps. Today we still look forward to hearing from reporters in other countries. We can even listen in on their chats with famous people!

1. What is the main idea of this story?
   a. **Edward R. Murrow was a brave American journalist.**
   b. Edward R. Murrow talked to many famous people.
   c. Edward R. Murrow worked in London.

2. What type of company did Murrow work for?
   radio station

3. What was special about Murrow's broadcasts in 1939?
   He broadcast live from London while it was being bombed.

4. How did people learn about the war before Murrow's work?
   through newsreels in movie theaters and newspaper articles

5. What does the story say caused modern reporters to interview famous people?
   Murrow's live interviews on television

6. Pretend you are a reporter. Ask someone for permission to be the subject of your interview. Prepare by writing out a number of questions in advance. Leave enough room after each question to record the answers. Choose a way to publish and share your interview.
   Check students' writing.

34   © Carson-Dellosa • CD-104621

Name _____ 3.RI.1, 3.RI.2, 3.RI.10

Finding Evidence
Read the story. Then, answer the questions. Underline evidence in the passage that supports your answers.

Elisha Otis

Have you ever ridden on an elevator? Elevators make it much easier for people to get from one floor to another in a tall building. At one time, elevators were not as safe as they are today. Elisha Otis helped change that. Early elevators used ropes. These ropes sometimes broke, sending the people riding the elevator to the ground. People could be hurt. Otis made wooden guide rails to go on each side of the elevator. Cables ran through the rails. The cables were connected to a spring that would pull the elevator back up if the cables broke. Otis displayed his invention for the first time at the New York Crystal Palace Exhibition in 1853. His safety elevators were used in buildings as tall as the Eiffel Tower in Paris, France, and the Empire State Building in New York City. Otis died in 1861. His sons, Charles and Norton, continued to sell his design, and many elevators today still have the Otis name on them.

1. What is the main idea of this story?
   a. The Otis family still sells elevators today.
   b. At one time, elevators were unsafe to use.
   c. **Elisha Otis found a way to make elevators safe.**

2. What are two buildings that used Otis's elevator design?
   the Eiffel Tower and the Empire State Building

3. You can tell a lot about people by what they say and do. Which sentence may have been said by Elisha Otis?
   a. **"I have an idea."**
   b. "Don't bother. It's probably good enough."
   c. "Just take the stairs."
   d. "Ropes are just as strong as cable."

4. Think of the times you have been in an elevator. Write a letter to Otis to thank him for making elevators safe. Describe some of the places where you have used an elevator. Use a computer to type your letter.
   Check students' writing.

© Carson-Dellosa • CD-104621   35

Name _____ 3.RI.1, 3.RI.2, 3.RI.10

Finding Evidence
Read the story. Then, answer the questions. Underline evidence in the passage that supports your answers.

Susan B. Anthony

You may know the name Susan B. Anthony from the U.S. dollar coin. But, Anthony was famous long before the coin was made. She was a leader who worked for women's rights in the 19th and 20th centuries. Anthony grew up in the Northeast of the United States. A teacher refused to teach her math because she was a girl. So, Anthony was educated at home. She became a teacher and fought for equal wages for women. Anthony attended a special meeting in New York, along with many others. She then began speaking publicly about women's rights. In 1869, Anthony and Elizabeth Cady Stanton formed a group. This was called the National Women's Suffrage Association. This group worked to gain women the right to vote. Anthony died in 1906. In 1920, the Nineteenth Amendment to the U.S. Constitution was passed. This finally gave American women the right to vote. Anthony was honored in 1979 with a dollar coin bearing her image.

1. What is the main idea of this story?
   a. Susan B. Anthony could not learn to do math.
   b. **Susan B. Anthony worked for women's rights.**
   c. A dollar coin honored Susan B. Anthony in 1979.

2. Why was Anthony educated at home?
   A teacher refused to teach her math

3. What did Anthony fight for as a teacher?
   equal wages for women

4. You can tell a lot about people by what they say and do. Which sentence may have been said by Susan B. Anthony?
   a. "We'll never be able to change the law."
   b. **"Come on, ladies! This is our right!"**
   c. "This is the way it has always been, so this is the way it should stay."
   d. "I'm so disorganized."

5. Think of the women you know. Think of how life would be different if women did not have the right to vote. Write a letter to Anthony to thank her for her work. Describe some of the women in your life and why you think it is important that they are able to vote. Use a computer to type your letter.
   Check students' writing.

36   © Carson-Dellosa • CD-104621

Answer Key

Finding Evidence

Read the story. Then, answer the questions. Underline evidence in the passage that supports your answers.

Thomas Edison

Without Thomas Alva Edison, we might all be sitting around in the dark! Although people before Edison worked on designs for the lightbulb, he is credited with creating the modern electric light. Edison was born in 1847. He worked as a telegraph operator. Edison liked working on the night shift so that he could have plenty of time to read and conduct experiments during the day. He invented the phonograph, or record player, in 1877. Edison built his own lab at Menlo Park, New Jersey. There he could continue to work on his inventions. The lab covered the space of two city blocks. Edison showed his lightbulb to the public in 1879. At this time, most people used candles to light their homes. The candles sometimes caused house fires. By 1887, over 100 power plants were sending electricity to customers. Edison registered over 1,000 patents. A patent is a design for an invention. It is no wonder that a newspaper called him the Wizard of Menlo Park!

1. What is the main idea of this story?

   Thomas Edison was a successful American inventor.

2. What are two of Edison's inventions?

   phonograph, lightbulb

3. Why did Edison like working on the night shift?

   plenty of time to read and conduct experiments during day

4. Circle the synonym that best replaces the word conduct in the following sentence:

   This gave him plenty of time to read and conduct experiments during the day.

   lead   pass   (perform)   run

5. You can tell a lot about people by what they say and do. Which sentence may not have been said by Thomas Edison?

   a. "How about trying this?"   b. "That might be a better way!"

   c. "I might need more space."   (d.) "Candlelight is so comforting."

6. Think of how life would be different if the modern lightbulb had not been invented. Write a letter to thank Edison for his invention. Use a computer to type your letter.

   Check students' writing.

Finding Evidence

Read the story. Then, answer the questions. Underline evidence in the passage that supports your answers.

Community Helpers

A community is a group of people. These people live in the same area or have the same interests. Communities need helpers to make them work. Some important community helpers are police officers. Police officers make sure everyone is following the rules of the community. They keep people safe. Firefighters are community helpers, too. Firefighters put out fires. They also educate people about fire safety. Other community helpers are people who work for the city. Garbage collectors help out. People put trash in bags or cans at the curb. Garbage collectors drive down city streets to pick up the trash. Park rangers help out, too. People play or have picnics in city parks. Park rangers make sure the parks are clean and safe. Another important helper in the community is a librarian. The librarian makes sure there are many good books available. Everyone in the community can use the library. The next time you see a community helper, say "Thank you!"

1. What is the main idea of this story?

   (a.) A community needs a lot of people to make it work.

   b. Police officers and firefighters are community helpers.

   c. People like to have picnics in city parks.

2. What do police officers do in a community?

   make sure everyone following the rules to keep people safe

3. Why does a community need park rangers?

   We need park rangers so that the parks are clean and safe to

   play or have picnics.

4. There are many other community helpers. Think of a community helper who has helped you or your family. Write a letter to thank this person. Describe how this person has affected your life. Use a computer to type your letter.

   Check students' writing.

Finding Evidence

Read the story. Then, answer the questions. Underline evidence in the passage that supports your answers.

Musical Cultures

People from different cultures celebrate different holidays. They eat different kinds of food. They also have different musical cultures. The United States has many musical traditions. People in New Orleans, Louisiana, in the southern part of the United States, are known for jazz. This music has strong rhythms. Jazz allows people to play freely. People from a region of the eastern United States called Appalachia play folk music with fiddles and banjos. Much of this music is based on the songs and dance tunes of the British Isles. Countries that border each other have music styles from the people who cross from one country to the other. Some styles from Mexico are banda and cumbia. Some Canadian styles of music are based on French songs. These styles use accordions and guitars. Because of the radio and television, people all over the world can hear music of other cultures and create new musical traditions of their own.

1. What is the main idea of this story?

   a. Different cultures have different holidays and food.

   b. Some Canadian music is based on French songs.

   (c.) People have different musical cultures.

2. What is jazz?

   a style of music from New Orleans with strong rhythms that lets

   people play freely

3. What are some styles of music from Mexico?

   banda, cumbia

4. How do radio and television affect musical cultures?

   They let people hear music from all over the world and create

   new music of their own.

5. What is your favorite kind of music? What types of instruments do you like listening to? Do you create music yourself? Write a letter to a famous musician describing what you like about music. Use a computer to type your letter.

   Check students' writing.

Finding Evidence

Read the story. Then, answer the questions. Underline evidence in the passage that supports your answers.

World Holidays

You and your family may celebrate many special days a year. People all over the world recognize different holidays. Some people in China have a Lantern Festival. This festival celebrates the new year. They light special lamps and hold colorful parades through the streets. In Scotland, some people celebrate Burns Night. This holiday honors the Scottish poet Robert Burns. It falls on his birthday. Families or clubs gather together. They eat a special meal. Then, they read Burns' poetry. Americans celebrate their independence on Independence Day. Canadians celebrate Canada Day on July 1 because the government of Canada was created on that day in 1867. On both Canada Day and Independence Day, people have parades and picnics. People in some parts of Germany celebrate Oktoberfest. This festival marks the harvest. They eat traditional German foods like sausage and potato salad. People who move to other countries carry their traditions to their new homes. This is why many places outside of those countries celebrate the same holidays.

1. What is the main idea of this story?

   a. Burns Night is a special holiday in Scotland.

   (b.) People around the world celebrate different holidays.

   c. Oktoberfest takes place in many cities.

2. How do people in Scotland honor Robert Burns?

   eat a special meal on his birthday, read his poetry

3. How are Independence Day and Canada Day celebrations alike?

   community parades, picnics

4. What does Oktoberfest represent?

   the harvest

5. Why might someone take their traditions to a new country?

   Answers will vary

6. Think of three special holidays that you celebrate. Write a letter to a pen pal from another country describing these holidays. Use a computer to type your letter.

   Check students' writing.

Answer Key

Elijah McCoy

Name _____   3.RI.2, 3.RI.4, 3.RI.10

Vocabulary
Read the story. Then, answer the questions.

Elijah McCoy

You may have heard something referred to as "the real McCoy." This saying means "the real thing" instead of a copy. Some people think that "the real McCoy" was Elijah McCoy, who was born in Canada in 1843. His parents were former slaves who escaped from Kentucky to Canada. At the time, slavery was illegal in Canada but not in the United States. McCoy traveled to Scotland when he was 16 to learn how to design, build, and repair machines. After the US Civil War ended, he moved to Michigan, where he worked on the railroad. He had to pour oil into the engine whenever the train stopped. McCoy worked on inventions in his home machine shop. He came up with the idea for a device to keep train engines oiled. His invention helped trains run more smoothly. Railroad workers would ask for "the real McCoy" because it was better than other machines like it.

1. What is the main idea of this story?
   a. Elijah McCoy created a tool to keep train engines running smoothly.
   b. Elijah McCoy was "the real McCoy" that the saying refers to.
   c. Elijah McCoy spent several years in Scotland.

2. What does the phrase *the real McCoy* mean?
   the real thing instead of a copy

3. You can tell a lot about people by what they do. Circle the adjective(s) that you think describe Elijah McCoy. Use a dictionary if necessary.
   fearful   (industrious)
   (innovative)   tired

4. Is there something you use that you would want "the real McCoy" for as well? Why? On a separate sheet of paper, describe what you would want. Support your opinion with several reasons.
   Check students' writing.

© Carson-Dellosa • CD-104621   41

Name _____   3.RI.2, 3.RI.4, 3.RI.10

Vocabulary
Read the story. Then, answer the questions.

Sandford Fleming

What time is it? Before the work of Sandford Fleming, it could be hard to tell. Fleming was born in Scotland in 1827. He moved to Canada to work on the railway. He drew up plans for a railroad from the east coast to the west coast. He worked to promote the use of iron bridges rather than wood. Fleming thought iron bridges were safer. In 1851, he designed the first Canadian postage stamp. It was worth three cents and had a picture of a beaver on it. In 1876, Fleming was traveling in Ireland. He missed his train. The schedule said that it would leave at 11 o'clock in the evening. Instead, the train left at 11 o'clock in the morning. Fleming knew how to avoid this kind of problem. He suggested that countries around the world use a single 24-hour clock. By 1929, most of the world's countries had adopted time zones that fit into this standardized time measurement.

1. What is the main idea of this story?
   a. Sandford Fleming was Scottish but lived in Canada.
   b. Sandford Fleming came up with the idea for standardized time.
   c. Sandford Fleming missed a train in Ireland.

2. You can tell a lot about people by what they do. Circle the adjective(s) that you think describe Sandford Fleming. Use a dictionary if necessary.
   (conscientious)   (inventive)
   (precise)   sloppy

3. What does the story say was the effect of Fleming missing his train?
   He invented standardized time.

4. In the final sentence of this story, what does the word *adopted* mean?
   a. taken into their homes
   b. legally become part of a family
   c. started to use
   d. rejected

5. Use a map or the Internet to learn about time zones. How did Fleming's ideas change the way people tell time today? Write a paragraph on a separate sheet of paper.
   Check students' writing.

42   © Carson-Dellosa • CD-104621

Name _____   3.RI.2, 3.RI.4, 3.RI.10

Vocabulary
Read the story. Then, answer the questions.

Harriet Tubman

Harriet Tubman was a brave woman. Tubman grew up as a slave in Maryland. She escaped north to Philadelphia, Pennsylvania, as an adult. Tubman returned to Maryland to help rescue her family. She returned again and again to help other slaves. Tubman guided them to safe houses along a network known as the Underground Railroad. People who helped slaves move to safety were called "conductors." These conductors were named after the people who controlled trains on railroads. In 1861, the United States began fighting the Civil War. Part of the struggle between the northern states and the southern states was about whether people should be allowed to own slaves. In 1863, President Abraham Lincoln signed a law stating that slavery was no longer allowed in the United States. With the law on her side, Tubman continued to help people who were treated unfairly. She died in 1913.

1. What is the main idea of this story?
   Harriet Tubman helped people on the Underground Railroad.

2. What did people in Tubman's time believe about slavery?
   Many people believed that slavery was wrong, but some Americans still owned slaves.

3. What does the phrase *Underground Railroad* mean in this story?
   a. a subway system   b. a hidden railway
   c. a secret system of safe houses   d. a secret passageway

4. You can tell a lot about people by what they do. Circle the adjective(s) that you think describe Harriet Tubman. Use a dictionary if necessary.
   (courageous)   meek   (resourceful)   content

5. Why do you think Tubman kept returning to help other slaves?
   Answers will vary.

6. Use reference books or the Internet to learn about the Underground Railroad. On a separate sheet of paper, write a paragraph describing the Underground Railroad and how it was used.
   Check students' writing.

© Carson-Dellosa • CD-104621   43

Name _____   3.RI.2, 3.RI.4, 3.RI.10

Vocabulary
Read the story. Then, answer the questions.

Flags of the World

A flag tells something special about an area or a group. Look at the US flag. The 13 stripes are for the first 13 states. The stripes are red and white. The 50 stars are for the current 50 states. The stars are on a blue field. Look at the Canadian flag. It has a red maple leaf on white between two bands of red. The maple leaf stands for the nature found in Canada. Canadian provinces and U.S. states also have their own flags. The state flag of Texas has a large white star on blue on the left and two bands of red and white on the right. Because of the flag's single star, Texas is called the Lone Star State. The flag of the Canadian province of New Brunswick has a gold lion on a red field above a sailing ship. The lion stands for ties to Brunswick, Germany, and the British king. The ship represents the shipping industry. The United Nations is a group of countries that works for world peace. It has a flag, too. Its flag shows a globe surrounded by olive leaves, which are a symbol of peace.

1. What is the main idea of this story?
   a. Flags tell something special about a country or group.
   b. Some flags have maple leaves or lions on them.
   c. Many flags are red, white, or blue.

2. Why is Texas called the Lone Star State?
   the state flag has one star

3. What does the word *field* mean in this story?
   a. an area of grass
   b. a large area of a single color
   c. an area of study

4. Use an encyclopedia or the Internet to look at different countries' flags. On a separate sheet of paper, design a flag to represent your school. Carefully choose colors, shapes, and other symbols. Describe these symbols on a second sheet of paper. Include your reason for choosing it.
   Check students' writing.

44   © Carson-Dellosa • CD-104621

© Carson-Dellosa • CD-104621   113

Answer Key

Name _____

3.RI.2, 3.RI.4, 3.RI.10

Vocabulary
Read the story. Then, answer the questions.

City Government

A president is a key national leader. So is a prime minister. There are also important leaders in your city. Many cities have a mayor. The mayor goes to events like the opening of a new library or a parade. The mayor often works with the city council. This is a group of people from areas all over the city. They work together to solve problems that will help all citizens. A city may also have a manager. The city manager makes sure that city services are running smoothly day-to-day. This person also creates a budget. The budget shows how the city should spend its money. There are many other members of city government. They include the chief of police and the fire chief. These people lead the police and fire departments. They make rules that their employees must follow. A city needs many workers to make a better life for everyone.

1. What is the main idea of this story?
   a. The president is an important leader.
   b. The leader of the police is called a chief.
   c. City government includes many different workers.

2. What does a city manager do?
   makes sure city services are running smoothly, creates a budget

3. What is a *budget*?
   a. a report that tells how the city should spend its money
   b. a city manager
   c. a person who leads the fire department

4. Why does a city need many workers?
   to make a better life for all of its citizens

5. Think about your school. You and your classmates are citizens. The teachers, custodians, and other staff are workers as well as citizens. On a separate sheet of paper, make a chart showing your school's organization. Start at the top of the page. Draw a circle for the principal. Then draw other circles for other jobs. Label the circles.
   Check students' writing.

© Carson-Dellosa • CD-104621   45

Name _____

3.RI.2, 3.RI.4, 3.RI.10

Vocabulary
Read the story. Then, answer the questions.

The Olympic Games

People from all over the world take part in the Olympic Games. They gather together to compete in different sports. The original Olympics were held in Greece around 776 BCE. They occurred every four years. Young men ran races of different lengths. Winners were given wreaths of olive branches. The modern Olympics resumed in 1896. That year, they were held in Greece. In 1996, people decided to split the Olympic Games. Now the summer and winter Olympics are held separately. The Olympics now occur every two years. People from more than 200 countries compete in either summer or winter sports. Today's winners receive gold, silver, or bronze medals. They compete in hundreds of events. The Olympics are good for the host countries, too. It gives them a chance to show off their culture. Both the people who attend and the people who watch on TV learn about the host country. The sports may differ from the original Olympics, but the spirit of goodwill and good sportsmanship is still the same.

1. What is the main idea of this story?
   a. The Olympics are held every four years.
   b. People come to the Olympics to compete in different sports.
   c. Good sportsmanship is very important at the Olympics.

2. When and where were the first Olympics held?
   in Greece around 776 BCE

3. How do the Olympics help people learn about different cultures?
   Answers will vary.

4. Two athletes have just won gold and silver at the Olympics. What are they thinking? Write your answer from the point of view of each athlete. Use complete sentences.
   Gold medal winner: **Check students' writing.**
   Silver medal winner: _____

5. The author uses the word *culture* in this story. Culture can include a lot of things about a group of people. What does it NOT include?
   a. music   b. language   c. clothing   d. air

6. Make a Venn diagram on a separate sheet of paper. On one circle, put your favorite sport. On the other circle, put another sport. Compare and contrast the differences and similarities between the sports.
   Check students' writing.

46   © Carson-Dellosa • CD-104621

Name _____

3.RI.2, 3.RI.4, 3.RI.10

Vocabulary
Read the story. Then, answer the questions.

Cleaning Up Earth

We have many cities to live in. But, we have only one Earth. We cannot move to a new one. So, it is important to take care of our planet. You may have heard the phrase "Reduce, reuse, recycle." Putting these words into action will help keep Earth clean. First, reduce the amount of waste you make. Cook with fresh fruits and vegetables instead of packaged foods. Second, reuse things when you can. Don't throw that milk carton in the trash. Make a bird feeder from it instead! Have you got extra clothes? Don't toss them out. Donate them! Finally, recycle plastic, glass, metal cans, and paper. These materials can be turned into new items to sell. Then they won't clog up a landfill. Practice "reduce, reuse, recycle." If we all work together, Earth will be a cleaner, better place for years to come.

1. What is the main idea of this story?
   a. Keeping Earth clean is important for everyone.
   b. Fresh vegetables taste better than packaged ones.
   c. Earth has too much trash.

2. Describe the differences between reduce, reuse, and recycle.
   reduce—use less; reuse—use again; recycle—turn materials into new items

3. How can you reduce the amount of waste you produce?
   Answers may vary.

4. Think of new ways to help to clean up Earth. Write your ideas in complete sentences on a separate sheet of paper. Try to come up with at least three ways each of reducing, reusing, and recycling. Share your work with friends. Try to follow through on at least one of these ideas.
   Check students' writing.

© Carson-Dellosa • CD-104621   47

Name _____

3.RI.2, 3.RI.4, 3.RI.10

Vocabulary
Read the story. Then, answer the questions.

The Continents

Earth is divided into seven large areas of land. These areas are called continents. The seven continents are Asia, Africa, Australia, Europe, Antarctica, North America, and South America. Each continent is separated from the others by a landform such as an ocean or a mountain range. Continents may be divided into many smaller areas as well. These areas are called countries, states, or provinces. People live on six of the seven continents. The continent of Antarctica is at the South Pole. The weather here is too cold for people to live. Some scientists study at the South Pole at special stations, but many stay there for only part of the year. The largest continent is Asia. Asia covers over 17,000,000 square miles (44,000,000 square km). The smallest is Australia, which covers nearly 3,000,000 square miles (7,700,000 square km). Asia also has the most people. Its population is over three billion. That accounts for about half the world's people!

1. What is the main idea of this story?
   a. More people live in Asia than on any other continent.
   b. It is hard for people to live in Antarctica.
   c. Continents are large areas of land on Earth.

2. What separates continents from each other?
   features such as oceans or mountain ranges

3. What is a station in the story?
   a. a place where scientists study
   b. an area of the classroom
   c. a television channel

4. Why do you think that so many people live in Asia?
   Answers may vary.

5. At the top of a separate sheet of paper, write "My Home." Divide the page into two sections. On the left side, start a list by writing the name of the largest place in which you live: Earth. Leave two blank lines underneath. Then write the name of the next largest place in which you live: North America. Leave two more blank lines. Continue down the page until you reach the smallest place: your room or home. Use the right side of the page to write two complete descriptive sentences about each particular place.
   Check students' writing.

48   © Carson-Dellosa • CD-104621

Answer Key

Vocabulary

Read the story. Then, answer the questions.

Planning a City

What do the streets in your city look like? Some cities have streets that are very straight and organized. It is easy to get from one point in the city to another. Other cities have streets that seem to go nowhere. It may be difficult to give directions to your home. When a group of people move to a place and start setting up the streets, they may use something called a grid system. One example of this is found in the city of Philadelphia, Pennsylvania, which is divided into four sections around a central square. The map was laid out by William Penn in 1682. The grid included wide streets that were easy for people to walk down. Penn left London, England, after a fire destroyed most of the city. London had a maze of narrow streets that were hard to move around in. Penn wanted to make sure people could get around the city easily and safely. Many other cities followed Penn's ideas when setting up their street systems.

1. What is the main idea of this story?
   a. William Penn drew the first grid system.
   (b.) Planning a city is important for safety.
   c. Some streets are straight and organized.

2. What is one good thing about having straight streets?
   Answers may vary.

3. What is a *grid system*?
   a way of arranging straight streets in a city

4. Why did Penn leave London?
   because a fire destroyed most of the city

5. How are Philadelphia's streets different from London's?
   Philadelphia has wide streets set up on a grid system, while
   London's streets are narrow and hard to move around.

6. What kind of street do you live on? Is it busy or quiet? Is it wide or narrow? Is it paved or gravel? Write a paragraph on a separate sheet of paper describing the streets in your neighborhood.
   Check students' writing.

Vocabulary

Read the story. Then, answer the questions.

Magnets

A magnet is any object with a magnetic field. This means that it pulls things made of iron, steel, or nickel toward it. If you set a paper clip next to a magnet on a table, the paper clip will move toward the magnet. Every magnet has what is called a north pole and a south pole. The north pole of one magnet will stick to the south pole of another magnet. If you try to push the south poles of two magnets together, they will spring apart. Earth has magnetic poles too. Earth is a big magnet! Earth's magnetic poles are not actual places. They are areas of Earth's magnetic field with a certain property. Although Earth's magnetic poles are different than the poles like the one where polar bears live, its magnetic poles are near these poles. The north pole of a magnet will always try to point toward Earth's north magnetic pole. A compass is a piece of camping equipment that shows direction. It has a magnetized needle. This needle points to Earth's magnetic north pole. So, if you get lost, pull out your compass and set it on a flat surface. Wait for the needle to point north.

1. What is the main idea of this story?
   a. If you get lost in the woods, start walking north.
   b. Compasses work by pointing to the north.
   (c.) Magnets are objects that have magnetic fields.

2. What happens if you push two south poles together?
   spring apart

3. In the phrase, *north pole of a magnet*, what does the word *pole* mean?
   a. the part that is attached to a tall post or tree
   (b.) the part that will always point toward Earth's north magnetic pole
   c. positive
   d. negative

4. Use an encyclopedia or the Internet to learn about the history of the compass. Compare these first compasses to the compass you would take on a camping trip today. Write your answer in the form of a paragraph on a separate sheet of paper. Use the computer to publish your writing. Share your research.
   Check students' writing.

Vocabulary

Read the story. Then, answer the questions.

Reptiles and Amphibians

You may think that lizards and frogs are in the same family. They're not! They are actually quite different. Lizards, snakes, turtles, and crocodiles are reptiles. Frogs, toads, and salamanders are amphibians. Both amphibians and reptiles are cold-blooded. Cold-blooded animals depend on their surroundings for their body temperature. Most amphibians and reptiles lay eggs instead of giving birth to their young. Reptiles lay hard-shelled eggs in nests. Amphibians lay soft-shelled eggs underwater. When reptiles hatch, they look like tiny adults. Amphibian babies might not. Baby frogs, called tadpoles, have to live underwater until they are older. Reptiles feel dry and scaly to the touch. Amphibians feel moist and sticky. Adult amphibians spend their time both in water and on land. This makes amphibians more at risk for becoming sick from pollution. It is important to keep ponds and lakes clean so that the animals that live there will be safe.

1. What is the main idea of this story?
   (a.) There are important differences between reptiles and amphibians.
   b. Reptiles are the same as amphibians.
   c. Frogs and lizards belong to different families.

2. How are amphibians and reptiles similar?
   cold-blooded, lay eggs

3. Why is it important to keep ponds and lakes clean?
   so the water is clean and keeps animals living there healthyw

4. Reread the first sentence of this story. What is another word or phrase with the same meaning as *family*?
   a. related siblings
   b. geckos and toads
   c. parents or grandparents
   (d.) related species

5. Choose one amphibian and one reptile. Use an encyclopedia or the Internet to learn about these animals. Use your research to compare them. Write your answer in the form of a paragraph on a separate sheet of paper. Use the computer to publish your writing. Share your research.
   Check students' writing.

Vocabulary

Read the story. Then, answer the questions.

Solid, Liquid, Gas

All matter on Earth exists in one of three states: solid, liquid, or gas. Solids, such as boxes or books, have a certain shape that is hard to change. Liquids, such as lemonade or orange juice, take the shape of the bottle or cup they are in. Gases, such as the air you breathe, spread out to fill the space they are in. It is easy to change water from one state to another. The water that you drink is a liquid. When water is heated, such as in a pot on the stove, it becomes a gas. This gas is known as steam, or vapor. Steam is used in an iron to make clothes smooth. It also can be used in a large machine to make electricity. When water is frozen, such as in a tray in the freezer, it turns into ice. Ice is used to cool down drinks or to help a hurt part of the body heal.

1. What is the main idea of this story?
   a. Steam is heated water.
   (b.) All matter exists as a solid, liquid, or gas.
   c. Ice cubes make water taste better.

2. What do you call water in the three states of matter?
   drinking water, ice, steam or vapor

Are the following sentences true or false? Write T or F in the space provided.

3. **F** Lemonade is a solid that takes the shape of its container.

4. **T** Your body is composed of solids, liquids, and gases.

5. Reread the first sentence of this story. What is another word or phrase with the same meaning as *states*?
   (a.) groups arranged by similarities
   b. provinces or countries
   c. groups arranged by nationality
   d. to say or announce

6. Think of three things: one solid, one liquid, one gas. Use your personal experience, or the Internet, to learn about these objects. Use your research to compare them. Think about how these things are used. Although they exist in different states, are there any similarities? Organize your research in the form of three paragraphs on a separate sheet of paper. Use the computer to publish your writing.
   Check students' writing.

Answer Key

Name _____

(3.RI.2, 3.RI.6, 3.RI.10)

Point of View
Read the story. Then, answer the questions.

Computers

Have you ever used a computer at school, at the library, or at home? Today's computers can fit on a desktop or in your lap. Computers of the past took up a whole room! One of the first computers was called the ENIAC, which stood for Electronic Numerical Integrator and Calculator. It took up 1,800 square feet (about 167 square meters), weighed nearly 50 tons, and cost $500,000. The ENIAC took three years to build and was designed for the U.S. Army. It required a team of six people to program it, or tell it what to do. The ENIAC was used from 1947 to 1955. In contrast, a personal computer today can weigh as little as two pounds (about one kilogram) and can be operated by one person at a time. The builders of the ENIAC may never have believed students could do their homework on a computer.

1. What is the main idea of this story?
   a. The ENIAC was an early computer.
   b. Computers of the past were very different from ones today.
   c. Students can do their homework on computers.

2. What does the word *program* mean in this story?
   a. build a computer
   b. require six people to use
   c. tell a computer what to do

3. How are computers today different from those of the past?
   smaller, lighter, and easier to use

4. How is your point of view about computers different from the author of the passage?
   Answers will vary.

Name _____

(3.RI.2, 3.RI.6, 3.RI.10)

Point of View
Read the story. Then, answer the questions.

Food Webs

A food web is a drawing that shows how different living things are connected. On the web drawing, it shows which animals at the top eat the animals directly below them, and so on until the bottom of the web. For example, a food web might start at the bottom with plants like grass and nuts, which do not eat other living things. Above these plants might be small animals such as mice and insects. Larger animals like owls and snakes eat the smaller animals. A food web can tell you what might happen if different plants or animals disappear from an ecosystem, or the surroundings in which all of these things live. In the food web described above, if something happened to the grass, then the mice and insects would not have much food. This would affect the owls and snakes, which would also not have enough food. Soon, there would be fewer of every animal. This is why it is important to protect all living things in an ecosystem, not just the largest ones.

1. What is the main idea of this story?
   a. Food webs show how all living things are connected.
   b. Owls and snakes are the most important animals.
   c. Only the animals at the top should be protected.

2. What is an ecosystem?
   a. a food web for very large animals
   b. the surroundings where a group of plants and animals live
   c. a place that grows only grass and nuts

3. A food web is a cause and effect chain. In the story, what might contribute to, or cause, a decrease in the owl population?
   Answers will vary.

4. Answer the following question in a complete sentence, written from that animal's point of view.
   How does the food web affect my life?
   Mouse: **Check students' writing.**
   Snake: _____

5. Write the name of a small plant or insect at the bottom of a separate sheet of paper. Use research from an encyclopedia and the Internet to draw a food web starting from this plant or insect. Continue up your food web as many levels as possible. Display your food web in your class and discuss your findings.
   Check students' writing.

Name _____

(3.RI.2, 3.RI.6, 3.RI.10)

Point of View
Read the story. Then, answer the questions.

Floods

Rain is good for people and plants. We need rain. But when it rains too much, people may be in danger. Flash floods are dangerous. They occur when a lot of rain falls very quickly. The rain fills up the streets faster than the water can drain away. It is very risky to drive in a flash flood. Your car may be swept away. If you live in an area where flooding is likely, listen to the radio or television when it starts to rain. The newscaster may tell you to move to a higher location. Be ready to leave your home. Before you leave, turn off all electrical equipment. Move important items to a higher floor, if possible. If you leave on foot, do not walk through moving water. Do not drive through standing water unless it is less than six inches (15.24 cm) deep. After a flood, listen to news reports again. The newscaster will tell you when you can return home and when the water from your tap will be safe to drink.

1. What is the main idea of this story?
   a. Flash floods can be dangerous and happen suddenly.
   b. Never drive through a flooded area.
   c. Take important items with you when you leave your home.

2. When should you leave your home?
   if the newscaster tells you to move to a higher location

3. What should you do before leaving your home?
   turn off all electronics and move important items to a higher floor

4. What might contribute to, or cause, a car to be swept away? Write your answer in a complete sentence.
   Answers will vary.

5. In this story, the phrase "standing water" means:
   a. water with feet   b. flowing water   c. still water   d. drinkable water

6. How does the author feel about rain? Is this the same or different than your point of view about rain? On a separate sheet of paper, write a paragraph explaining your point of view.
   Answers will vary.

Name _____

(3.RI.2, 3.RI.6, 3.RI.10)

Point of View
Read the story. Then, answer the questions.

Silkworms

Silk is a soft, smooth type of cloth that is used for clothing, bedding, and wall hangings. It comes from silkworm cocoons, which are spun into thread that is then made into cloth. It takes about 3,000 cocoons to make one pound (about 0.5 kg) of silk. Silkworms become moths as adults. Like most insects, silkworms go through four stages. The moth lays its eggs on a mulberry leaf. After a silkworm hatches into a caterpillar, it munches on leaves until it grows to the length of a human finger. After about a month of eating and growing, the worm spins a cocoon of silk around itself. Spinning the cocoon takes about three days. Inside the cocoon, the silkworm changes shape and becomes a pupa. After about three weeks, the pupa turns into a moth. The moth comes out of the cocoon and starts the cycle all over again.

1. What is the main idea of this story?
   a. Silkworm cocoons are spun into thread.
   b. Silkworms turn into moths as adults.
   c. Silkworms go through four stages and help make silk.

2. What are the stages of a silkworm's life?
   egg, caterpillar, pupa, moth

3. The word *stage* can have several meanings. Which sentence uses stage in the same way as the author of this story?
   a. The school auditorium has a huge stage.
   b. The actors will stage a play in December.
   c. My baby sister is at a crawling stage.
   d. My friend likes to dance on the stage.

4. Use an encyclopedia or the Internet to learn more about the silkworm. Write a description of the silkworm's life cycle from its point of view. Use a computer to type your work.
   Check students' writing.

Answer Key

3.RI.2, 3.RI.6, 3.RI.10

Point of View
Read the story. Then, answer the questions.

Science Experiments

Scientists learn about the world by conducting experiments. They take careful notes on the supplies they use and the results they find. They share their findings with others. This leads to everyone learning a little more. You can do experiments too! The library has many books with safe experiments for students. You might work with balloons, water, or baking soda. You might learn about how light travels. You might find out why marbles roll down a ramp. Ask an adult to help you set up your experiment. Let them watch to make sure you are being safe. Be sure to wash your hands afterward. And, remember to clean up the area. Take good notes on your work. You may be able to change just one thing the next time. This might give you a completely different result. Do not worry if your results are not what you expected. Some of the greatest scientific discoveries were made by mistake!

1. What is the main idea of this story?
   (a.) Children can do experiments too, as long as they are safe.
   b. Scientists often make mistakes that lead to great discoveries.
   c. You should always take good notes when conducting an experiment.

2. Where can you find information about safe experiments?
   the library, or on the Internet

3. Should you worry if you get different results? Why or why not?
   some of the greatest scientific discoveries were made by
   mistake

4. Which sentence(s) do you think a good scientist would NOT say?
   (a.) "I don't have to write that down. I'm sure I will remember it."
   b. "I should double-check my measurements."
   (c.) "I'm not going to bother to measure this water."
   (d.) "It worked once, so I don't have to do it again."

5. What is the author's point of view about science experiments? How do you know? Explain your answer on a separate sheet of paper.
   Answers will vary.

© Carson-Dellosa • CD-104621   57

3.RI.2, 3.RI.6, 3.RI.10

Point of View
Read the story. Then, answer the questions.

Glaciers

A glacier is a large, thick mass of ice. It forms when snow hardens into ice over a long period of time. It might not look like it, but glaciers can move. They usually move very slowly. However, if a lot of the ice melts at once, the glacier may surge forward, or move suddenly over a long distance. Most glaciers are found in Antarctica, the continent at the South Pole, or in Greenland, which is near the North Pole. Areas with glaciers receive a lot of snowfall in the winter. They have cool summers. Most glaciers are located in the mountains, where few people live. Sometimes they can cause flooding in cities and towns. Falling ice from glaciers may block hiking trails farther down on the mountain. Icebergs are large floating pieces of ice. Icebergs may break off from glaciers and cause problems for ships at sea.

1. What is the main idea of this story?
   a. Icebergs can be dangerous to ships.
   (b.) Glaciers are large masses of ice found mainly in the mountains.
   c. People usually live far from glaciers.

2. Where are most glaciers found?
   mountains of Antarctica and Greenland

3. What is the weather like where glaciers are found?
   winters have a lot of snowfall, summers are cold

4. How can glaciers be dangerous?
   Answers will vary.

5. The word *surge* means to flow in waves or bursts. Which sentence does not use *surge* correctly?
   a. The sudden surge of electricity caused the power to go out.
   b. The library flooded in that storm surge.
   c. He surged forward on the last lap and won the race.
   (d.) The clock surged in a regular tick-tock rhythm.

6. How do you feel about glaciers after reading the passage? Did the author's point of view change your opinion? Why or why not? Explain your answer on a separate sheet of paper.
   Answers will vary.

58   © Carson-Dellosa • CD-104621

3.RI.2, 3.RI.7, 3.RI.10

Visual Aids
Read the story. Then, answer the questions.

Tornadoes

A tornado is a funnel cloud that forms over land. It is created when warm air meets cold air. This makes a thunderstorm. Tornadoes can be very dangerous to both people and things. They can leave a trail of damage one mile (1.6 km) wide and 50 miles (80 km) long. The wind speed can reach over 300 miles (480 km) per hour. People often have little warning of a tornado, but certain parts of the United States have tornadoes more often than other parts. There is an area called "Tornado Alley". It covers parts of Texas, Oklahoma, Kansas, Nebraska, Iowa, and South Dakota. Tornadoes are more likely to form in the spring and summer. If the weather reporter says that a tornado has been spotted in your area, stay inside. Go to the lowest level of your home. Keep as many walls as possible between you and the outside. Keep the windows closed. Do not leave until you hear that the tornado has passed.

1. What is the main idea of this story?
   a. Tornadoes are formed during thunderstorms.
   b. Tornado Alley is an area where many storms occur.
   (c.) Tornadoes are dangerous to people and buildings.

2. When are tornadoes more likely to form?
   spring and summer

3. What illustration (e.g., diagrams, photographs) would help you understand this story better? How?
   Answers will vary.

4. You are a weather reporter. You must warn your listeners about a tornado. You need to report the tornado's movements and remind people how to protect themselves. Write your report on a separate sheet of paper. Use a dictionary or thesaurus to help make your report more dramatic. Then, read your report aloud to your class.
   Check students' writing.

© Carson-Dellosa • CD-104621   59

3.RI.2, 3.RI.7, 3.RI.10

Visual Aids
Read the story. Then, answer the questions.

Sea Urchins

Sea urchins look like pincushions that live under the sea. They have long, thin spines that stick out all over their bodies. Most sea urchins have spines that are about 0.39 to 1.18 inches (1 to 3 cm) long. Sea urchins are found in oceans all over the world. They can be many colors, from green to brown to red. Their bodies are about 4 inches (10 cm) across. They eat dead fish, seaweed, and very tiny plants called algae. Their spines help them trap food. They also use their five tiny teeth to pull plants off rocks. Hundreds of tiny tubes used as feet help them move along the seafloor. Many creatures, including sea otters, crabs, and eels, like to eat sea urchins.

1. What is the main idea of this story?
   (a.) Sea urchins are interesting animals that live in the ocean.
   b. Sea urchins taste salty and creamy.
   c. Sea urchins look like pincushions.

2. How do sea urchins move?
   They have hundreds of tiny tubes used as feet.

3. How do sea urchins pull plants off rocks?
   They use their five tiny teeth.

4. What illustration (e.g., diagrams, photographs) would help you understand this story better? How?
   Answers will vary.

5. You are a spokesperson for an aquarium. You want people to come see all the animals, not just the dolphins and penguins. On another sheet of paper, create an advertisement persuading people to visit the sea urchins. Use an encyclopedia or the Internet to discover more interesting facts. Share your ad with the class.
   Check students' writing.

60   © Carson-Dellosa • CD-104621

Answer Key

Visual Aids

Read the story. Then, answer the questions.

Health and Fitness

Health and fitness are very important for young people. If you start good habits now, you have a better chance of being a healthy adult later. You may go to gym class several times a week, but you should also try to stay fit outside of school. You and your family can make healthy choices together. You can choose fresh fruit for dessert instead of cake. Offer to help make dinner one night and surprise your family by preparing a delicious salad. You can go for a walk together after dinner instead of watching television. Exercising can help wake up your brain so that you can do a good job on your homework. Making healthy choices may seem hard now, but after a while it will feel good.

1. What is the main idea of this story?
   a. Going to gym class is fun.
   b. Making healthy choices is too hard.
   c. Health and fitness are important for you and your family.

2. Where should you try to stay fit?
   outside of school

3. How does exercise affect your brain?
   It wakes up your brain so that you can do your homework.

4. What does the story say may contribute to becoming a healthy adult?
   good habits

5. The word *fit* has several meanings. Which one of these sentences uses *fit* in the same way as in the story?
   a. The house is a good *fit* for Grandpa because it is close to the golf course.
   b. We had to bring our dog to the vet because he was having a *fit*.
   c. That marathon runner must really be *fit*!
   d. The plumber *fit* the new piece onto the pipe.

6. Would an illustration (e.g., diagrams, photographs) help you understand this story better? Why or why not? Explain your answer on a separate sheet of paper.
   Answers will vary.

Opinion Writing

Look at the list of words below. Write each word in the correct list.

Sports

bases	goalie	mound	pool
dive	goggles	pass	score
glove	kick	pitcher	swimsuit

Swimming	Soccer	Baseball
pool	**score**	**mound**
swimsuit	**kick**	**bases**
dive	**goalie**	**pitcher**
goggles	**pass**	**glove**

Imagine a coach has asked if you are interested in playing one of the sports listed above. On a separate sheet of paper, answer in the form of a letter written to the coach. Explain why you do or don't want to play that sport. Use at least 3 words from the list in your letter. Your letter should contain at least four complete sentences.

Check students' writing.

Opinion Writing

Look at the list of words below. Write each word in the correct list.

Weather

blazing	mittens	splash	thunder
hot	puddle	summer	umbrella
icy	shovel	swimming	winter

Sunny	Snowy	Rainy
summer	**mittens**	**umbrella**
blazing	**icy**	**puddle**
swimming	**winter**	**splash**
hot	**shovel**	**thunder**

What type of weather do you like best? On a separate sheet of paper, explain why you like this type of weather. In the second paragraph, explain what you don't like about other types of weather. Use at least 6 words from the list.

Check students' writing.

Opinion Writing

Look at the list of words below. Write each word in the correct category.

Senses

barking	eyelid	noise	radio
concert	glasses	perfume	skunk
cookies	lemon	picture	watch

Sight	Hearing	Smell
watch	**radio**	**skunk**
picture	**concert**	**lemon**
glasses	**noise**	**perfume**
eyelid	**barking**	**cookies**

On a separate sheet of paper, explain how you use your sense of sight, hearing, and smell. Use at least nine words from the list. In your conclusion, state which sense you believe people use the most. Give reasons to support your opinion.

Check students' writing.

Answer Key

Informative Writing

Look at the list of words below. Write each word where it is most commonly found.

Animals

elephant	hamster	lion	rabbit
giraffe	kangaroo	penguin	turtle
goldfish	kitten	puppy	zebra

Pets   **Zoo Animals**

kitten	**hamster**	**penguin**	**lion**
goldfish	**turtle**	**zebra**	**elephant**
puppy	**rabbit**	**kangaroo**	**giraffe**

Pick an animal from the lists. Use an encyclopedia or the Internet to research more about this animal. On a separate sheet of paper, write a short paragraph describing your animal. Add illustrations to make your description clearer.

Check students' writing.

Informative Writing

Look at the list of words below. Write each word where it is most commonly found.

Food

cereal	fruit	peas	salad
dumplings	juice	pizza	sausage
fish	pancakes	rice	toast

Breakfast   **Dinner**

toast	**cereal**	**fish**	**salad**
sausage	**juice**	**rice**	**dumplings**
pancakes	**fruit**	**pizza**	**peas**

On a separate sheet of paper, describe what you might eat for breakfast and dinner. Organize your work into two short paragraphs, one for each meal. Use at least 6 words from the list. Add illustrations to make your description clearer.

Check students' writing.

Informative Writing

Look at the list of words below. Write each word where it is most commonly found.

Rooms

apron	dishwasher	hangers	stove
blanket	flour	pajamas	teapot
clothes	fork	slippers	toys

Bedroom   **Kitchen**

slippers	**clothes**	**dishwasher**	**teapot**
pajamas	**hangers**	**stove**	**apron**
toys	**blanket**	**fork**	**flour**

On a separate sheet of paper, describe a bedroom and kitchen. Organize your work into two paragraphs. Use at least 9 words from the list. Add illustrations to make your descriptions clearer.

Check students' writing.

Narrative Writing

Look at the list of words below. Write each word in the correct list.

Time

awake	daylight	moonlight	sleep
bedtime	dusk	noon	sunlight
dawn	midnight	school	sunset

Day   **Night**

sunlight	**dawn**	**midnight**	**sleep**
daylight	**awake**	**moonlight**	**bedtime**
sunrise	**noon**	**dusk**	**sunset**

Choose an imaginary character, such as a pirate, an elf, or a unicorn. Write a short story from your new point of view to describe a day (or a night) in your life. Include at least 3 words from the list. Use dialogue to help describe your feelings and thoughts. After revising, read your story aloud to your family or friends.

Check students' writing.

Answer Key

Narrative Writing

Look at the list of words below. Write each word in the correct list.

Extreme Places

anchor	camel	sandstorm	thirsty
beach	lighthouse	scorpions	tide
cactus	oasis	seagulls	waves

Ocean

anchor	**tide**
beach	**waves**
lighthouse	**seagulls**

Desert

cactus	**sandstorm**
camel	**scorpions**
oasis	**thirsty**

Imagine being lost at sea in a small boat, or wandering through a desert on foot. Write a short story written to describe your adventure. Your story should include at least 4 words from the list. Use dialogue to help describe your feelings and thoughts. After revising, read your story aloud to your family or friends.

Check students' writing.

Narrative Writing

Look at the list of words below. Write each word in the correct list.

Dream Vacation

astronaut	comet	gravity	peak
climb	avalanche	orbit	spacesuit
cold	galaxy	oxygen	towering

Visiting the Moon

astronaut	**gravity**
comet	**spacesuit**
galaxy	**orbit**

Climbing Mount Everest

climb	**towering**
cold	**peak**
avalanche	**oxygen**

Your Uncle Pete has invited you on vacation. You can blast to the moon, or you can climb the tallest mountain in the world. Your only human companion will be Uncle Pete. Write a short story to describe your adventure. Your story should include at least 5 words from the list. Describe actions and events as they happen. Use dialogue to help describe your feelings and thoughts. After revising, read your story aloud to your family or friends.

Check students' writing.

Word Endings

Fill in the blank with the word that makes the most sense in the sentence. It may be helpful to cross off the words in the word bank as they are used.

bet	net	pet	set	vet	wet

1. Lucas has a **pet** rabbit.
2. We had to take our sick dog to the **vet** .
3. My stepdad hit a tennis ball over the **net** .
4. Please **set** the dishes on the table.
5. I **bet** my brother will sleep late tomorrow.
6. Hope's hair was **wet** after she washed it.

best	nest	pest	quest	vest	west

7. The birds made a **nest** in the tree.
8. I wore my favorite **vest** to school.
9. Sam is on a **quest** to find his book.
10. My family drove from east to **west** last summer.
11. The bee was a **pest** buzzing around Shara's head.
12. I got the **best** math grade in the class.

Word Endings

Fill in the blank with the word that makes the most sense in the sentence.

brake	flake	lake	wake

1. I caught a **flake** of snow in my hand.
2. Joseph showed me how to use the **brake** on my bike.
3. June and Jude went fishing at the **lake** .
4. Sometimes, it is hard to **wake** up in the morning.

back	snack	pack	sack

5. Ben helped put the food in a **sack** at the store.
6. The three boys sit at the **back** of the bus.
7. I am hungry for a **snack** .
8. My stepmom will **pack** our car for the trip.

page	age	stage	wage

9. The actors stood on the **stage** .
10. Your **age** tells how old you are.
11. Anna's job pays a good **wage** .
12. Turn the **page** and begin reading the next chapter.

Answer Key

Word Endings

Fill in each blank with a word from the -eck family that makes the most sense in the sentence.

1. My cat has a white **fleck** on her left paw.
2. Put a **check** next to the correct answer.
3. A **speck** of dirt is on my shirt.
4. The bird likes to **peck** at her food.
5. Captain Shaw stood on the **deck** of the ship.

Fill in each blank with a word from the -ind family that makes the most sense in the sentence.

6. Sasha is **blind**, yet she is an amazing piano player.
7. Always be **kind** to your neighbors.
8. The teacher stood **behind** the class for the photograph.
9. Liam peeled the **rind** off his orange.
10. Grandpa has to **wind** his watch.

Fill in each blank with a word from the -eal family that makes the most sense in the sentence.

11. Breakfast is the first **meal** of the day.
12. Is that a **real** story, or did you make it up?
13. Bandaging your elbow will help it **heal**.
14. The baseball player tried to **steal** third base.
15. You should **seal** an envelope before you mail it.

Word Endings

Fill in the blank with the word that makes the most sense in the sentence. It may be helpful to cross off the words in the word bank as they are used.

camp	damp	lamp	ramp	stamp	champ

1. I put a **stamp** on my letter.
2. Susan wheeled herself up the **ramp**.
3. The rain made the grass **damp**.
4. We love to **camp** by the river.
5. Uncle Quan turned on the **lamp** for more light.
6. The fastest runner became the **champ**.

bump	dump	jump	clump	pump	stump

7. My friend can **jump** high.
8. Julie put a **clump** of grapes on her dinner plate.
9. We took the trash to the city **dump**.
10. Cecilia used a **pump** to put air in her bike tires.
11. Watch out for the **bump** in the road.
12. The woodcutter chopped down the tree and left a **stump**.

Word Endings

Fill in the blank with the word that makes the most sense in the sentence.

hay	may	ray	tray

1. Mom, **may** I have some more grapes, please?
2. Horses like to eat **hay**.
3. Please take the **tray** of food to your table.
4. A **ray** of light shined on my pillow.

splash	dash	flash	mash

5. Bill likes to **splash** in the water.
6. A **flash** of lightning lit the sky.
7. Jill won the 50-yard **dash**.
8. Dad will **mash** potatoes for dinner.

sped	led	bred	fled

9. The lion almost caught the gazelles before they **fled**.
10. Carlos **led** during most of the race, but Jayla won.
11. Some kinds of dogs are **bred** to fetch things.
12. The police car **sped** to the accident.

Word Endings

Fill in the blank with a word from the -ight family that makes the most sense in the sentence.

1. We took a **flight** on an airplane to see Grandma.
2. Casey's old shoes are too **tight** to wear.
3. Our eyes give us the sense of **sight**.
4. Hilda shined the **bright** flashlight on the ground.
5. The empty box was very **light** to carry.

Fill in the blank with a word from the -ive family that makes the most sense in the sentence.

6. What time should we **arrive** for the party?
7. Zach and Katie saw their favorite singer **live** in concert.
8. The human body has **five** senses.
9. The bees buzzed around their **hive**.
10. Aunt Sharon will **drive** us to the game.

Fill in the blank with a word from the -aw family that makes the most sense in the sentence.

11. The ice will **thaw** if it gets warm outside.
12. The teacher will **draw** the winner's name out of a hat.
13. Don't break the **law** by speeding!
14. Beavers like to **gnaw** on trees with their big front teeth.
15. When they **saw** the new puppy, they wanted to keep it.

Answer Key

Name _____ 3.RL.4, 3.RF.3, 3.L.2

Word Endings

Fill in the blank with the word that makes the most sense in the sentence. It may be helpful to cross off the words in the word bank as they are used.

clip	drip	flip	sip	snip	trip

1. My dad can **flip** the pancakes in the pan.
2. Melting ice will **drip** in your hand.
3. Julio will **clip** the papers together.
4. The kitten likes to **sip** milk.
5. Jessica used scissors to **snip** the thread.
6. I am going on a **trip** to see Grandpa.

crop	drop	flop	mop	pop	stop

7. When I am tired, I **flop** onto my bed and rest.
8. I **stop** at the crosswalk and look both ways.
9. A **drop** of water fell into the sink.
10. The farmer planted his **crop** of wheat.
11. Liv needed to **mop** up the spill.
12. Please do not **pop** my balloon.

Name _____ 3.RL.4, 3.RF.3, 3.L.2

Word Endings

Fill in the blank with the word that makes the most sense in the sentence.

cream	dream	gleam	steam

1. The boiling water turned into **steam** .
2. My teeth always **gleam** after I visit the dentist.
3. Juan's **dream** is to become a teacher.
4. We had ice **cream** with our cake.

bow	cow	plow	how

5. The farmer had to **plow** the field.
6. This milk comes from a **cow** .
7. The actors took a **bow** .
8. George showed me **how** to boil eggs.

brain	gain	grain	pain

9. When my arm broke, I was in **pain** .
10. Bread is made from **grain** .
11. I use my **brain** to spell words.
12. As the puppy eats more, he will **gain** weight.

Name _____ 3.RL.4, 3.RF.3, 3.L.2

Word Endings

Fill in the blank with a word from the -ace family that makes the most sense in the sentence.

1. Mei walked away at a quick **pace** .
2. Someday, I want to go to outer **space** .
3. At bedtime, you should wash your **face** .
4. Go back to the **place** you started.
5. Angelo did not leave a **trace** of food on his plate.

Fill in the blank with a word from the -are family that makes the most sense in the sentence.

6. We paid our **fare** on the train.
7. A **hare** is like a rabbit.
8. Don't you **dare** touch that stove!
9. Please keep your **bare** feet off the furniture.
10. A female horse is called a **mare** .

Fill in the blank with a word from the -out family that makes the most sense in the sentence.

11. I heard someone **shout** , "Fire! Fire!"
12. Gavin put the water pail under the **spout** and began to pump.
13. I think the rainbow **trout** is the most beautiful fish in the world.
14. We will learn **about** caterpillars today.
15. A pig's **snout** is round and flat.

Name _____ 3.RL.4, 3.L.1, 3.L.4

Compound Words

A compound word is two words that have been put together to make a new word. For example, *thumb* and *print* can be put together to make the new word *thumbprint*. Look at each list of compound words. Fill in each blank in the stories below with the best compound word. Use each word once. Use capital letters when necessary.

necktie	earrings	briefcases	everyone
raincoats	necklace	stepmother	shoelaces

Getting Ready for the Day

Everyone in my family gets ready for the day in a different way. My **stepmom** puts on her jewelry like her **earrings** and a **necklace** . Dad puts on a **necktie** . They both pick up their **briefcases** to take to work. I just tie my **shoelaces** , and I am ready to go! When the weather is bad, we all do one thing the same. We all put on our **raincoats** .

suitcases	takeoff	doorway	headphones
airport	gumball	headband	airplane

Flying

Last year, Mom and I flew to visit Grandpa. We got to the **airport** early and put tags on our **suitcases** . When the **airplane** arrived, we got in line to board. We walked through the **doorway** of the airplane and found our seats. I took off my **headband** , and Mom gave me some **headphones** so that I could listen to music. After **takeoff** , my ears hurt a little, so Mom gave me a **gumball** to chew.

Answer Key

Name _____
(3.RL.4, 3.L.1, 3.L.4)

Compound Words

Look at the list of compound words. Fill in each blank in the stories below with the best compound word. Not all of the words will be used.

| butterflies | rosebush | backyard | fireflies | everywhere | flytrap |
| earthworms | stinkbug | ladybugs | honeybees | rainstorm | beeline |

Insects

Bugs are **everywhere** you look. **Honeybees** like to get pollen from flowers. **Butterflies** have colorful wings. **Ladybugs** are red with black spots. **Earthworms** live in the ground and come out after a **rainstorm**. When it is dark, **fireflies** come out and fly around. It is fun to see them light up in the **backyard**.

| underwater | catfish | castoff | rowboat | something | shoreline |
| fishhook | campfire | dockyard | sunshine | waterproof | shipwreck |

Fishing

My uncle likes to go fishing. He puts on old clothes and **waterproof** boots and stands by the water. Sometimes, he goes out in a **rowboat**. He puts bait on the **fishhook** and throws out the line. The hook sinks **underwater**. He waits for the **catfish** to take the bait. He stands in the **sunshine** and fishes until he catches **something**. Then, he cooks the fish over a **campfire**.

Name _____
(3.RL.4, 3.L.1, 3.L.4)

Compound Words

Look at the list of words. Fill in each blank in the stories below with the best compound word that you can create from the list. Use each word once.

| beat | cakes | fish | grand | pan | summer | time | up |
| bed | every | gold | mother | room | thing | tub | wash |

My Grandmother

I like it when my **grandmother** comes to stay with me in the **summertime**. She is an **upbeat** person. She knows how to make **everything** fun. She tells me stories while we make **pancakes** in the morning. We splash each other when she shows me how to wash clothes in a **washtub**. She sings funny songs while we feed my **goldfish**. Grandmother even knows games that make **bedroom** fun!

| ball | foot | head | knee | off | pads | some | times |
| down | gear | kick | news | over | paper | time | touch |

Football

My brother is on the **football** team. He wears special **kneepads** and **headgear** to keep his body safe. I go to watch his games **sometimes**. It is fun to watch the **kickoff** at the beginning of the game. One day, the game went into **overtime** and they had to play longer. My brother scored the winning **touchdown**! The next day, his picture was in the **newspaper**!

Name _____
(3.RL.4, 3.L.1, 3.L.4)

Compound Words

Compound words are two words that have been put together to make a new word. For example, *eye* and *lid* can be put together to make the new word *eyelid*. Look at the list of compound words. Fill in each blank in the stories below with the best compound word. Use each word once.

| rainstorms | forecast | snowstorms | snowmen |
| rainwater | snowflakes | rainfall | thunderclouds |

Rain and Snow

The weather **forecast** tells us what weather we can expect. In the spring, we usually have **rainstorms** with lots of dark **thunderclouds**. Our garden needs the **rainfall**, and we like to collect **rainwater** to water our plants with later. During winter, we usually get **snowstorms**! We watch the white **snowflakes** fall. Later, we go outside and play in the snow. We even make **snowmen**!

| someday | schoolteacher | anything | lawmaker |
| shoemaker | firefighter | hairdresser | salesperson |

Jobs

What job would you like to have **someday** when you are an adult? A **shoemaker** makes and fixes shoes. A **schoolteacher** works with children. A **hairdresser** cuts people's hair. Both a police officer and a **firefighter** help people. A **salesperson** sells things. A **lawmaker** works in an office. You can be **anything** you choose!

Name _____
(3.RL.4, 3.L.1, 3.L.4)

Compound Words

Look at the list of compound words. Fill in each blank in the stories below with the best compound word. Not all of the words will be used.

| classroom | lunchtime | seesaw | breakfast | popcorn | hallway |
| friendship | backpack | paperweight | bookmark | homework | playground |

My School Day

Mom wakes me up to get dressed and eat **breakfast**. I pack my **backpack** and go to school. I work at my desk in the **classroom**. When it is **lunchtime**, I sit with my friends. At recess, we go to the **playground**. We like to play on the **seesaw**. At the end of the day, our teacher writes our **homework** on the board. After school, I like to eat **popcorn** for a snack.

| nighttime | outside | ballgame | dogwood | nutshells | butterfly |
| bluebird | lunchtime | backyard | doghouse | playmate | weekend |

Weekend Fun

I like the **weekend** because I get to spend time **outside** with my dog Rusty. In the morning, Rusty comes out of his **doghouse** to play. We play in the **backyard** until **lunchtime**. Rusty likes to bark at the **butterfly** that lives in the garden. He also likes to chew on the **nutshells** that squirrels have dropped from the trees. When **nighttime** comes, Rusty and I are ready to sleep!

Answer Key

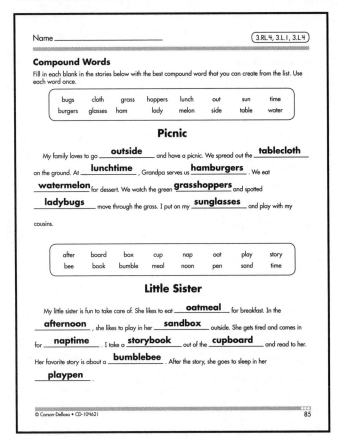

Compound Words

Fill in each blank in the stories below with the best compound word that you can create from the list. Use each word once.

bugs	cloth	grass	hoppers	lunch	out	sun	time
burgers	glasses	ham	lady	melon	side	table	water

Picnic

My family loves to go **outside** and have a picnic. We spread out the **tablecloth** on the ground. At **lunchtime**, Grandpa serves us **hamburgers**. We eat **watermelon** for dessert. We watch the green **grasshoppers** and spotted **ladybugs** move through the grass. I put on my **sunglasses** and play with my cousins.

after	board	box	cup	nap	oat	play	story
bee	book	bumble	meal	noon	pen	sand	time

Little Sister

My little sister is fun to take care of. She likes to eat **oatmeal** for breakfast. In the **afternoon**, she likes to play in her **sandbox** outside. She gets tired and comes in for **naptime**. I take a **storybook** out of the **cupboard** and read to her. Her favorite story is about a **bumblebee**. After the story, she goes to sleep in her **playpen**.

Homophones

> **Homophones** are words that sound alike but are spelled differently. The words also mean different things.

Choose the correct homophone for each sentence.

course	coarse	groan	grown

1. My uncle's beard is very **coarse**.
2. When I am fully **grown**, I want to be a nurse.
3. The pain in my leg made me **groan**.
6. Of **course** you may have more soup!

stare	stair	read	red

5. I sat on the bottom **stair** in front of the building.
6. Our teacher **read** a story to us after lunch.
7. My cat likes to **stare** out the window.
8. Ling wore a bright **red** dress in the play.

Homophones

Choose the correct homophone for each sentence.

one	won	here	hear	hire	higher

1. We are **here** to learn.
2. My brother hopes they **hire** him for the job.
3. David had **one** sticker left, and he gave it to his friend.
4. The plane flew **higher** than the kite.
5. Do you **hear** a band playing music?
6. Chan ran fast and **won** the race.

know	no	meet	meat	pause	paws

7. My cat washes her face using her **paws**.
8. Maria added **meat** to the taco.
9. Did you **know** that ice is frozen water?
10. The students will **meet** after school to play games.
11. Please **pause** so I do not miss anything.
12. There are **no** apples left on the tree.

Homophones

Choose the correct homophone for each sentence.

due	dew	seas	pair	pear	reign
do	seize	sees	pare	rain	rein

1. The fisherman sailed the seven **seas**.
2. A fun thing to **do** is to visit the creek.
3. Sherry's library book is **due** on Monday.
4. Josh **sees** his grandparents every weekend.
5. When you **seize** something, you grab it.
6. We smelled the morning **dew** in the air.
7. The king will **reign** for his whole life.
8. When you have a **pair** of something, you have two of them.
9. The cool **rain** felt good on our hot faces.
10. To make the horse slow down, pull on the **rein**.
11. Would you like an apple or a **pear**?
12. Mom will **pare** the potatoes before cooking them.

Answer Key

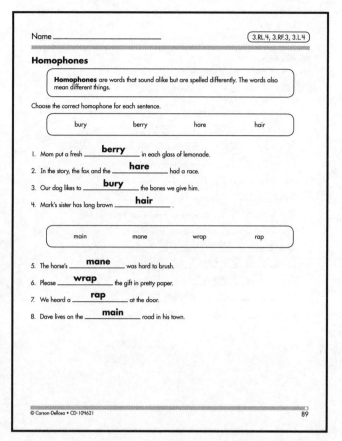

3.RL.4, 3.RF.3, 3.L.4

Homophones

Homophones are words that sound alike but are spelled differently. The words also mean different things.

Choose the correct homophone for each sentence.

| bury | berry | hare | hair |

1. Mom put a fresh **berry** in each glass of lemonade.
2. In the story, the fox and the **hare** had a race.
3. Our dog likes to **bury** the bones we give him.
4. Mark's sister has long brown **hair** .

| main | mane | wrap | rap |

5. The horse's **mane** was hard to brush.
6. Please **wrap** the gift in pretty paper.
7. We heard a **rap** at the door.
8. Dave lives on the **main** road in his town.

© Carson-Dellosa • CD-104621   89

3.RL.4, 3.RF.3, 3.L.4

Homophones

Choose the correct homophone for each sentence.

| right | write | sail | sale | root | route |

1. The **root** of a tooth is below the gum.
2. Mark the **right** answer on your paper.
3. Captain Juan will **sail** the boat to shore.
4. The sign says that the car is for **sale** .
5. Lilly liked taking the faster **route** to school.
6. I will **write** a story about my town.

| our | hour | side | sighed | weather | whether |

7. We will be home in an **hour** .
8. The **weather** is beautiful today!
9. Taylor **sighed** when she sat in her chair.
10. My family loves **our** house.
11. Sheila painted one **side** of the fence purple.
12. Harry wondered **whether** or not he should take an umbrella.

90   © Carson-Dellosa • CD-104621

3.RL.4, 3.RF.3, 3.L.4

Homophones

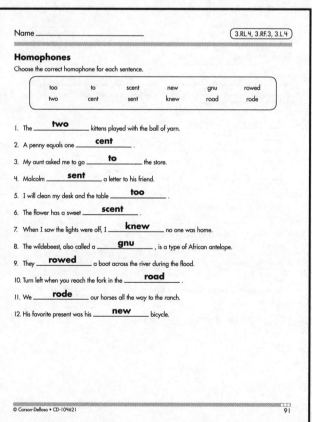

Choose the correct homophone for each sentence.

| too | to | scent | new | gnu | rowed |
| two | cent | sent | knew | road | rode |

1. The **two** kittens played with the ball of yarn.
2. A penny equals one **cent** .
3. My aunt asked me to go **to** the store.
4. Malcolm **sent** a letter to his friend.
5. I will clean my desk and the table **too** .
6. The flower has a sweet **scent** .
7. When I saw the lights were off, I **knew** no one was home.
8. The wildebeest, also called a **gnu** , is a type of African antelope.
9. They **rowed** a boat across the river during the flood.
10. Turn left when you reach the fork in the **road** .
11. We **rode** our horses all the way to the ranch.
12. His favorite present was his **new** bicycle.

© Carson-Dellosa • CD-104621   91

3.RL.4, 3.RF.3, 3.L.4

Homophones

Homophones are words that sound alike but are spelled differently. The words also mean different things.

Choose the correct homophone for each sentence.

| beach | beech | hoarse | horse |

1. I think I'm getting a cold because my throat is **hoarse** .
2. Grandpa had to cut down both the elm tree and the **beech** tree.
3. My **horse** loves to gallop.
4. My feet are sandy after playing at the **beach** .

| roll | role | I | eye |

5. My friend and **I** ate lunch together.
6. Would you like some butter on your **roll** ?
7. The **role** of the queen was played by Janna.
8. The pirate wore a patch over one **eye** .

92   © Carson-Dellosa • CD-104621

© Carson-Dellosa • CD-104621

Answer Key

Homophones

Choose the correct homophone for each sentence.

bare	bear	heel	heal	tale	tail

1. Joey hurt the **heel** of his foot when he stepped on a stone.

2. My favorite **tale** is the story about Jack and the giant.

3. A **bear** lives in the woods and likes to eat honey.

4. Doctors try to **heal** people.

5. Kurt stuck his **bare** feet in the swimming pool.

6. Her dog wags its **tail** when it is happy.

fair	fare	maid	made	weak	week

7. 1. My family went to the state **fair** .

8. What is your favorite day of the **week** ?

9. A **maid** is someone who helps with cleaning and serving.

10. After Uma won the race, her legs felt **weak** .

11. The bus **fare** is one dollar.

12. Katya **made** a picture frame for her stepdad.

Homophones

Choose the correct homophone for each sentence.

or	oar	vein	not	naught	teas
ore	vane	vain	knot	tees	tease

1. It was hard to row the boat with only one **oar** .

2. I think Nadia is **vain** because she is always looking at herself in the mirror.

3. A weather **vane** points in the direction the wind is blowing.

4. Dad wasn't sure if Teddy **or** I scored that goal.

5. When you give blood, the nurse will put a needle in your **vein** .

6. Miners dig for **ore** because it is a valuable rock that contains metal.

7. I told you, I am **not** going to leave you behind!

8. My brother likes to **tease** me, even though I don't like it.

9. Tito stopped to untie the **knot** in his shoelace.

10. Hot black and green **teas** are very popular to drink.

11. Another word for zero is the word **naught** , which means nothing.

12. My dad must have at least a hundred **tees** in his golf bag!

Context Clues

> When you come to a word and you do not know the meaning, use **context clues** to help you figure it out. Context clues are the other words around the word you do not know.

Use context clues to figure out the meaning of each underlined word below. Circle the correct meaning. Use a dictionary to help as needed.

1. My <u>style</u> is to wear T-shirts and jeans, but my sister wears fancy dresses.
   - a. clothes
   - **b. fashion**
   - c. boots

2. I <u>avoid</u> eating snacks before dinnertime.
   - **a. stay away from**
   - b. love
   - c. try to have

3. Lucy's family <u>permits</u> her to walk home with a friend.
   - a. bans
   - b. drives
   - **c. allows**

4. The <u>journey</u> from my house to Grandma's takes five hours.
   - **a. trip**
   - b. airplane
   - c. car

5. My brother built a <u>model</u> airplane. Then, he painted it red and blue.
   - a. real
   - b. person who shows off clothes
   - **c. toy**

6. Everyone loves her friendliness and <u>charm</u>.
   - a. voice
   - **b. nice manner**
   - c. necklace

7. Please <u>notify</u> the coach today if you would like to try out for the team.
   - **a. tell**
   - b. obey
   - c. play for

Context Clues

> Remember, use context clues to figure out the meaning of unknown words.

Use context clues to figure out the meaning of each underlined word below. Circle the correct meaning. Use a dictionary to help as needed.

1. The car tire scraped the <u>curb</u> as it went around the corner.
   - **a. edge of a road**
   - b. sidewalk
   - c. boots

2. We went on a <u>march</u> through the neighborhood.
   - a. month
   - b. band
   - **c. walk**

3. After Jerry ate the <u>entire</u> pizza, his stomach hurt.
   - **a. whole**
   - b. wheel
   - c. small

4. Polar bears live in <u>arctic</u> weather.
   - a. very hot
   - b. rainy
   - **c. very cold**

5. My stepmom is helping me study so I can <u>improve</u> my grades.
   - a. study
   - **b. raise**
   - c. read

6. My teacher invites families to <u>observe</u> her class so that they know how she teaches.
   - **a. watch**
   - b. leave
   - c. teach

7. The <u>motion</u> of the rocking boat made me feel ill.
   - a. ocean
   - b. captain
   - **c. movement**

8. The motor is at the <u>rear</u> of the boat, just behind the seats.
   - a. side
   - **b. back**
   - c. middle

Answer Key

Name _____

(3.RL.4, 3.RF.4, 3.L.4)

Context Clues

Use context clues to figure out the meaning of each underlined word below. Circle the correct meaning. Use a dictionary to help as needed.

1. The principal reason for studying is to learn new things.
   - **(a. main)**
   - b. school
   - c. last

2. The teacher will accept our homework until tomorrow morning.
   - a. stay away from
   - b. give away
   - **(c. take)**

3. We tried all morning, but it was impossible to get tickets to the game.
   - a. certain
   - b. easy
   - **(c. not possible)**

4. Mr. Loy told us the good news with a grin on his face.
   - a. cheerful
   - **(b. smile)**
   - c. sad

5. Joey put the photograph in a silver frame.
   - **(a. picture holder)**
   - b. question
   - c. snapshot

6. What is your individual opinion about the food?
   - a. class
   - **(b. own)**
   - c. thought

7. My uncle is a soldier in the military.
   - **(a. armed forces)**
   - b. officer
   - c. government

8. Corrie chose the ordinary name Spot for her Dalmatian puppy.
   - a. unusual
   - **(b. normal)**
   - c. correct

9. One element of a successful day is getting enough sleep.
   - a. start
   - b. chemical
   - **(c. part)**

Name _____

(3.RL.4, 3.RF.4, 3.L.4)

Context Clues

When you come to a word and you do not know the meaning, use **context clues** to help you figure it out. Context clues are the other words around the word you do not know.

Use context clues to figure out the meaning of each underlined word below. Circle the correct meaning. Use a dictionary to help as needed.

1. Marcy wanted to magnify the words on the bottle so that she could see them better.
   - **(a. make bigger)**
   - b. copy
   - c. read

2. Each person is wearing a label with his or her name on it.
   - a. jacket
   - b. shirt
   - **(c. tag)**

3. It is not nice to tease people or animals.
   - a. obey
   - b. talk to
   - **(c. bother)**

4. When water is heated, steam rises into the air.
   - **(a. droplets)**
   - b. ice
   - c. lakes

5. Mr. Jones conducts the choir when they give a concert.
   - a. behavior
   - **(b. leads)**
   - c. does experiments

6. It is always nice to see a familiar face.
   - a. unknown
   - b. belonging to parents
   - **(c. something that is known)**

7. Our school's teachers want to educate all of their students.
   - **(a. teach)**
   - b. study
   - c. watch

Name _____

(3.RL.4, 3.RF.4, 3.L.4)

Context Clues

Remember, use context clues to figure out the meaning of unknown words.

Use context clues to figure out the meaning of each underlined word below. Circle the correct meaning. Use a dictionary to help as needed.

1. In North America, people vote to elect their leaders of government.
   - a. object to
   - **(b. choose)**
   - c. win

2. The majority of the class voted to have pizza instead of sandwiches for lunch.
   - **(a. most people)**
   - b. few people
   - c. teachers

3. My mom's greatest concern is that we get home safely.
   - a. rule
   - b. problem
   - **(c. worry)**

4. A bride often wears a veil on her head during a wedding.
   - **(a. net that goes over the face)**
   - b. long gown
   - c. flowers

5. You should always be civil to other students and teachers.
   - a. quiet
   - b. rude
   - **(c. polite)**

6. The new pool is private. Only people who live in that neighborhood can use it.
   - a. open
   - **(b. not public)**
   - c. fun

7. The scent of some flowers makes my nose itch.
   - a. sound
   - b. sight
   - **(c. smell)**

8. I will wrap a gift for Mario to open at his party.
   - a. buy
   - b. speak about
   - **(c. put paper around)**

Name _____

(3.RL.4, 3.RF.4, 3.L.4)

Context Clues

Use context clues to figure out the meaning of each underlined word below. Circle the correct meaning. Use a dictionary to help as needed.

1. The underwater current can be very strong in the ocean.
   - a. breeze
   - b. beach
   - **(c. flow)**

2. We thought long and hard before making a decision.
   - a. argument
   - **(b. choice)**
   - c. lesson

3. Everyone at the party was very merry.
   - **(a. happy)**
   - b. upset
   - c. small

4. Our teacher will display the class poster for the rest of the school to see.
   - a. tear up
   - b. throw away
   - **(c. show)**

5. After a brief speech from one of the actors, the play began.
   - a. quiet
   - **(b. short)**
   - c. noisy

6. The baby seized the rattle his mom was holding and waved it around.
   - a. hit
   - b. stared at
   - **(c. grabbed)**

7. My cat likes to stare out the window.
   - **(a. watch)**
   - b. step
   - c. bother

8. Mike's dog likes to bury everything in a pile of dirt in the backyard.
   - a. eat
   - **(b. cover)**
   - c. play with

9. It is always best to be honest in what you do and say.
   - a. be funny
   - **(b. tell the truth)**
   - c. lie

Answer Key

Context Clues

When you come to a word and you do not know the meaning, use **context clues** to help you figure it out. Context clues are the other words around the word you do not know.

Use context clues to figure out the meaning of each underlined word below. Circle the correct meaning. Use a dictionary to help as needed.

1. Before it rains, I can feel the <u>moisture</u> in the air.
   a. thunder
   b. sunshine
   c. wetness

2. The <u>bark</u> on a tree is very rough.
   a. outer covering
   b. leaves
   c. sand

3. I <u>groaned</u> when I realized that I had forgotten my book.
   a. shouted
   b. whispered
   c. sighed loudly

4. My sister <u>beamed</u> when our mother said, "Good job!"
   a. shined a ray of light
   b. smiled broadly
   c. frowned

5. The <u>fare</u> for riding the train was a dollar for adults.
   a. ticket price
   b. store
   c. railroad

6. The crowd <u>rumbled</u> like thunder as the news spread.
   a. jumped
   b. screamed
   c. roared

7. My hand felt <u>weak</u> after I finished writing the report.
   a. strong
   b. tired
   c. loose

Context Clues

Remember, use context clues to figure out the meaning of unknown words.

Use context clues to figure out the meaning of each underlined word below. Circle the correct meaning. Use a dictionary to help as needed.

1. Dad likes to make a special tomato <u>sauce</u> to put on our pizza.
   a. bowl
   b. dinner
   c. topping

2. Drop the noodles into the pan when the water starts to <u>boil</u>.
   a. stir
   b. heat
   c. freeze

3. My mom and stepfather had to sign a special <u>form</u> to buy our house.
   a. paper
   b. book
   c. name

4. After I finished eating, my plate was <u>bare</u>.
   a. large animal
   b. empty
   c. plenty

5. I <u>like</u> wearing skirts because they are pretty when I twirl.
   a. spin
   b. don't like
   c. enjoy

6. The surface of the water was <u>calm</u> until it began to rain.
   a. stormy
   b. still
   c. wavy

7. Khalil liked the <u>glory</u> of winning the city's big race.
   a. honor
   b. flag
   c. medal

8. My friend and I are <u>opposites</u>, but we still have fun together.
   a. happy
   b. exactly alike
   c. not alike

Context Clues

Use context clues to figure out the meaning of each underlined word below. Circle the correct meaning. Use a dictionary to help as needed.

1. Shelby is on a <u>quest</u> to find her watch.
   a. wheel
   b. race
   c. search

2. Two world wars were fought during the 20th <u>century</u>.
   a. season
   b. period of 100 years
   c. month

3. The first 13 U.S. states formed a <u>union</u> so that they could be stronger.
   a. separation
   b. president
   c. single governing body

4. In the story, the fox chased the <u>hare</u> across the field.
   a. rabbit
   b. frog
   c. something on your head

5. In our <u>society</u>, everyone must follow certain laws.
   a. house
   b. community
   c. rules

6. Todd ate lunch in the <u>pause</u> between speakers.
   a. break
   b. animals' feet
   c. nap

7. Iesha <u>exclaimed</u> in a loud voice, "I got an A on the test!"
   a. sang
   b. read
   c. shouted

8. Seth <u>glanced</u> at my friend across the classroom.
   a. words
   b. looked
   c. spoke

9. The <u>effect</u> of staying up all night was that I fell asleep at breakfast.
   a. result
   b. cause
   c. change

Congratulations!

receives this award for

_____

_____

Signed _____

Date _____

avoid	argue	arctic	accept
beam	began	babies	balance
cardinal	bury	brief	bought
civil	citizen	charm	century

© CD

concern	conduct	course	churches
current	decision	display	educate
effect	elect	element	familiar
fancy	elves	favorite	knives

© CD

glory	freedom	expensive	flour
hire	eventually	fortunate	groan
include	improve	impossible	honest
label	journey	instrument	individual

© CD

library	liquid	magnet	maid
knew	majority	national	metal
military	model	motion	notify
observe	official	opinion	opposite

© CD

pour	permit	pause	ordinary
politely	private	principal	prefer
scent	sauce	remember	government
society	separate	seize	science

soldier	stare	style	instrument
threw	tease	tortoise	tomatoes
union	unusual	vapor	veil
volume	slept	wrap	yesterday

© CD